Mrs.
Keith,
Thanks so much for
your love & support over
the years. May God
continue to bless you.

Blessings,
Sondra "Kay" Smith
May 20, 2009

Nakia's Gift

A Mother's Journey
from Misery to Ministry

Nakia's Gift

A Mother's Journey from Misery to Ministry

Sandra Kay Gordon, BRE
Carolyn M. McKanders, MSW

Foreword by
Reverend Kenneth James Flowers, M.Div.

Afterword
Matthew Parker, MA

*Priority*ONE
p u b l i c a t i o n s
Detroit, Michigan, USA

*Priority*ONE Publications
P. O. Box 725 • Farmington, MI 48332
(800) 596-4490 Nationwide Toll Free
E-mail: info@p1pubs.com
URL: http://www.p1pubs.com

ISBN 13:978-1-933972-16-9
ISBN 10:   1-933972-16-5

Edited by Paula Ester and Nina Wheeler

Cover design by Lori Block and Christina Dixon

Interior design by PriorityONE Publications

Printed in the United States of America

Praise for Nakia's Gift

To God be the Glory! I have watched Rev. Sandra Kay Gordon grow to be a wise and spiritual person. She is a loving and supportive wife, a caring mother and a friend to others. She is also God's faithful preacher. May God continue to bless her as she is moved by God's command.

Her loving husband,
Rev. Charles E. Gordon

My wife Carolyn McKanders and her friend Reverend Sandra Kay Gordon, two beautiful souls, are guided by God and Grace to provide this healing testimonial to Nakia and God's unconditional Love.

Kenneth McKanders

My precious god-daughter Nakia, you have been a precious gift from God. You were the one who loved life and life loved you, we thought. Your death was a tragedy to all, but not in vain. God has been able to take this adversity and turn it into a Blessing. Your mom and Carolyn were able to take this experience and minister to others in need. May God bless them and give them continuous strength.

Linda Bassett
Godmother

Praise for Nakia's Gift cont'd

Nakia's Gift captures the real essence of God's providence in bringing the two of you together. That he chose Nakia to make this possible is just a testimony of His sovereignty. Thank you for being obedient to His calling. Those who read this book, whether they are dealing with suicide or not, will be able to find healing from other hurts.

Theresa M. Doyle
(Sandra's sister, Carolyn's friend)

Nakia's Gift is a powerful story of God's unfailing love and power to transform us in the midst of tragedy. The death of a loved one is a painful experience. When that loved one's death is a result of suicide, the pain is beyond description. Gordon and McKanders begin this journey from hurt, disappointment, anger and fear to hope and healing. We see God's creative work through their experiences and we are reminded that our misery can certainly blossom into a beautiful ministry.

Rev. Lauren Ellis,

When tragedy strikes we seek to understand the reason, and many times there are no answers, at least none that will suffice. I thank God that Rev. Sandra Kay Gordon had help in the process of dealing with her tragedy. Not only did God step in, He also sent her a physical partner to assist in the healing process. Together, Rev. Gordon and Carolyn have created a written account of the healing process and I know it will serve to assist others in their journey. Glory to God!!!

Kimberly T. Flowers, RN, MA, LPC

Praise for Nakia's Gift cont'd

The journey described in *Nakia's Gift* is truly a blessing. Each step has allowed me to be ministered to personally. As I reflect upon my childhood friend I realize that the Gift we were given was Triumph, when all we saw in the beginning was tragedy. Enjoy and allow this book to minister to your soul. Also share it with others who may feel as though there is no one who is going through the pain. Thank God for Mrs. G, for having the strength to share her story to heal us all.

Minister Leon Morehead

Gordon and McKanders explore the "deep, rocky crevices" and pain associated with suicide. After Nakia's suicide, McKanders provided Gordon with the roadmap to emotional and spiritual healing.

Rosalind Whitehead

Table of Contents

Acknowledgments

Sandra K. Gordon

All praise and thanks be to God for the evolving and final completion of this book. It has been nearly seven years since Carolyn and I began writing; yet we know God's timing is perfect.

I especially want to thank my husband, Charles for his love and compassion for me as I journeyed through the stages of grief. He was always there for me, willing to listen or wipe my tears and sometimes just hugging me when all I could say is "I need a hug - I hurt." Despite dealing with his own grief, he found the time to be there for me. Thank you Charles!

To my children, Charles Jr. (C.J.) and Sandra Lynette for their determination to press on despite their tremendous pain over the loss of their sister. Also, to my stepchildren Tony and Carmen who were Nakia's big brother and sister, it is my prayer that you continue to hold on to your faith. I love you as if you were my own children.

To my father, Arthur Murphy, Jr., thank you for being a pillar of strength for me and for encouraging me to hold to my faith and belief that God would see me through my difficult times.

To my "twin cousin," Debralyn, who was responsible for giving Nakia her name. You have kept your promise to be there for me – thanks cuz.

To my spiritual niece Madelyn McCargo, I will never forget the bond God gave us as we journeyed together – waiting to come forth in our calls into ministry. You felt my pain intensely, which speaks clearly through your poems. May God forever bless you in all your endeavors.

I certainly want to say thank you to our editors, my sister Theresa Doyle; Carolyn's husband Ken; Rosalind Whitehead; and Candice Tomlinson, for your help and advice, and to Greater New Mt. Moriah Secretaries, Retha Williams and Bernadean-Boulware Yokley for pre-publication editing and typeset help.

No words can express the thanks and love I have for my Church family, the Greater New Mt. Moriah Missionary Baptist Church. You were truly there for me before and after the funeral. I often think of those days before the funeral and how someone was there at the house with me for 24/7. To the Department of Missions, their President, Dolores Christmas (I would awaken some mornings to find her sleeping on the floor); to Circle 14 and their chairperson my dear friend and Nakia's godmother, Linda Bassett who coordinated around the clock care for me and my family. To Constance Smith, who just stepped in and did things I didn't have the strength to do. Druel Outley, Naomi Ruff, Mary Carey, and Doris Perry thanks for being true sisters!

To my Pastor, Reverend Kenneth James Flowers for being there for me and my family; for continuing to believe in me and encouraging me to fulfill God's call on my life. Thanks for having enough faith in me that you hired me as your Assistant. I will always be grateful to God that you are my Father in the Ministry. Your confidence, trust and faith in me have been a source of strength for me. Thank You.

To our First Lady, but most especially my dear, dear friend and sister, Kimberly Tenine Flowers, thanks girl!! You were indeed my "other counselor," helping me through the rough times, listening to me, and spending time with me when I just needed a friend. God sometimes gives us friends just for a season, but I know that you are a lifetime friend and I thank God for you!

A special thanks to Joan MacMillan, Phyllis Borman and Mary Howard, my co-workers at the time. You shared my pain and made sure I didn't come home alone that day. Phyllis and Joan you will always be a special part of my life. I enjoy our dinner fellowships when we find time to get together.

Finally, to my counselor, Carolyn McKanders. You will always be "my counselor." WOW is all I can say. Although our counseling sessions have long ago ceased, it was those sessions that God used to bring about my healing. Thank you so much for being more than a counselor. Thank you for being willing to allow God to use you to help me. You have a special gift from God and many lives have been and will be touched because of your love for God and commitment to helping others. It took us seven years to finish this book; it has indeed been a blessed journey. As the both of us embark on other assignments God has given us, may we always find time to touch bases with each other because we are ON A JOURNEY! God bless you and may his anointing always rest upon you.

Acknowledgments

Carolyn McKanders

As Sandra and I navigated this divinely appointed journey, I was constantly aware of two forces: the awesome love and power of God and the unwavering support of my husband Ken, and my children. All glory to God and deep love and appreciation to my family.

The Foreword
by

The Reverend
Kenneth James Flowers, M.Div.

Suicide is a devastating phenomenon that wreaks havoc upon a grieving family. It causes deep feelings of guilt, hurt, shame, anger, resentment and fear. For when one takes one's life, his or her family is left to pick up the pieces and begin anew, even though numerous questions race through the family's mind like, "What could I have done to prevent this?" and "Why didn't I see it coming?"

Nakia's Gift: A Mother's Journey from Misery to Ministry is an excellent resource tool to overcome the pain and agony of losing a child to suicide. The Reverend Sandra Kay Gordon opens her heart and soul to the reader as she delves deep into her innermost feelings surrounding the suicide of her beloved daughter, Nakia, who took her life at the tender age of 23 years old. Nakia's death came at a time when Reverend Gordon was wrestling with her personal Call to Ministry. She struggled with whether to go forth or not, as well as the age-old question, "How will my husband and children deal with me being a Minister?" Thus, Nakia's suicide was a devastating blow to a woman's faith, who asked God, "Lord, Why?" Then there were the theological questions that had to be answered, i.e., "Will

Nakia be forgiven for taking her own life?", and "Is suicide an unforgivable sin?"

Moreover, in *Nakia's Gift*, Reverend Gordon becomes transparent to her readers by talking candidly about her personal hurt, pain and agony of not having her daughter with her any longer. She doesn't know how to stop the pain of missing her so much, especially on holidays. Gordon also discusses her guilty feelings and how she becomes angry with God and with everyone, including Nakia. Yet, her Spiritual Counselor/Therapist, Carolyn McKanders, will not allow Gordon to have a "pity-party." At the end of each chapter, McKanders gives her spiritual reflections, as well as her clinical response to Gordon's feelings of hopelessness and despair. It is she who tells Gordon that it is fine to be angry with God and angry with Nakia. Yet, she cannot allow her anger and resentment to consume her life and her spiritual well-being.

Subsequently, God does indeed speak to Reverend Gordon, who answers her Call to Ministry. A grieving Christian mother goes from **"Misery to Ministry,"** as she begins to cope better with her daughter's death. In reading this most powerful book, one will understand the fact that one must pray in order to get beyond the suicide of one's child in particular, or any person in general. One must also trust in the Lord to deliver him or her from the feelings of guilt, fear, anger, resentment, hurt, and loneliness. Finally, one must not be afraid to open up to a Spiritual Therapist, who is qualified to walk one through "the valley of the shadow of death." Thus, it is important to pray to God Almighty; and it is also important to seek counseling from a professional therapist/spiritual leader or Pastor.

Therefore, even though Nakia is gone, her precious Gift to her mother is to be an encourager, a motivator and even her Guardian Angel. Out of the pain and agony of Nakia's suicide, comes forth an anointed Minister of the Gospel, who has been appointed and approved by God. It's a Journey in which Reverend Gordon is still traveling. She is traveling to wholeness, health and happiness. On what Journey are you now traveling?

My Nakia

For nine months I carried you,
You were my first born
You blessed us with your beauty and smile
Little did I know,
That I would only have you a little while
The years went by...preschool,
Middle, then High,
Oh how the years did fly,
A new car, new job,
New beginnings for you,
Things seemed to be so bright
I tried so hard with all my might
To understand what happened
On July 15th that made you take your life
I don't try so hard any more
To figure it all out
I'm trusting God to show me
What to do to help others
Although I couldn't help you
So many people were left in so much pain
Carmen, Tony, C.J and Lynette-your siblings
Don't even understand

If only you could've felt
The love others had for you,
I'm certain it would've helped
To bring you through
So as the days and years go by, my Nakia,
Know each day I'll continue
To show my love for you
As God helps me, teaches me,
Shows me what to do,
Even when my heart aches
I know I will get through
Because of God's grace and
My constant love for you

Love Always,
Mom

Preface

Giving birth must be the most miraculous event to happen to a female. For me, carrying a child in my womb for nine months was simply awesome – I often pondered how awesome God must be that He designed birth to be this way. The doctors decided to induce my labor after a week long hospital stay because I was borderline toxemic. My labor was hard and long, but after 12 ½ hours I gave birth to my first child, Nakia Terese Gordon, on October 15, 1974. She weighed 6 pounds, 12 ½ ounces and was 19 ½ inches long. Of course, she was the most beautiful baby in the whole world!

To describe how Nakia was as a child is to envision a child who is full of life and always doing something. Nakia had a presence about her that seemed to catch other's attention when she walked into the room. Even during her toddler years, when she was shy around those she did not know, people would rave over her beauty, her eyes, and her smile. Nakia became a very proud child, very particular about her hair and her clothes. I remember Nakia learned to tie her shoelaces before turning three. She would press me daily to teach her how to tie her laces because she did not like for her shoelaces to become untied. In her early years, Nakia had very high self-esteem and an amazing faith in God. She believed God could do anything and she stood on what she believed. She was very popular in school and at church, having a lot of friends who always claimed her as their "best friend."

I don't know exactly when Nakia began to struggle with her self-esteem. I sometimes think it began in the fourth grade when she contracted ringworm from a student in her class. For six months, Nakia had to make bi-weekly visits to the dermatologist because the ringworm was in her hair. I could not use a hot comb or any chemicals in her hair, therefore, instead of wearing her hair straight, the way she preferred, it was very thick and bushy. Nakia was devastated and I am not sure if she ever recovered from the teasing of her fellow classmates. Although Nakia seemed fine most of the time, in retrospect, I believe there were indeed times when she struggled with her appearance. Most people thought Nakia to be a beautiful young lady, yet she would spend hours preparing for outings; her hair, nails and clothes had to be just right. Nakia attended Henry Ford High School half of the day and the other half was spent at Crockett Vocational Center where she was taking cosmetology classes. From her second year in high school until her death, I did not go to a hair salon. She would do my hair at home, practicing her different hairstyles on me. Although others and I thought that she was very good, Nakia never gained the confidence she needed to take the state board exams in order to receive her license.

Nakia was not the best student academically in high school, but I found out later that part of her problem was that she was a little too popular and would get side tracked and lose focus on her studies. However, she pulled her grades up enough to run for, and win, homecoming queen in her senior year of high school. What a joyous occasion that was for Nakia and how proud her family was of her!

After graduating from high school, Nakia maintained contact with several of her school friends. Our home was always busy with her friends (as well as Lynette and C.J's) visiting often. Nakia loved to "socialize", going out often with her friends and talking on the phone every free moment she had. Her days were full, working and then planning where to go and what to do. She seemed to love life. She also loved to travel and was not afraid to board a plane alone to go to visit her friend in Las Vegas or her aunt Melba in Maryland. I remember how excited she was when she returned from Maryland, telling me of the limousine rides she and her aunt had taken to tour the Washington, D. C. area.

Nakia seemed to have a lot going on for herself, having finally secured a job with a major company. Despite all the positive things Nakia had in her favor, she still seemed to struggle with her relationships with the opposite sex. She and I would have long talks about relationships and about life, in general. Our last major talk would be the Sunday before she died, when she and I sat and talked for nearly three hours about life, relationships, and her love for God. Little did I know that even then, she was masking her pain, not really letting me know the emotional state of her despair. I thought she and I had "good open honest talks" yet, her pain, she kept to herself – a secret she let no one in on, not even me.

Introduction

Sandra K. Gordon

It's hard to know exactly where to begin, so I'll start with a brief synopsis of my life after January 26, 1997. This was the day that I accepted my call into the ministry to preach the Gospel. My journey was not an easy one, but that is another book in the making. After accepting my call, I began what seemed to be a long and tedious journey before I preached my first sermon at Greater New Mt. Moriah Missionary Baptist Church. Many things occurred from January 26, 1997 until December 30, 1998; however, the most painful thing that happened was the loss of my daughter, Nakia Terese Gordon.

On July 15, 1998, my first-born and my husband's third, used a 410 rifle to kill herself. This was the most horrible day of our lives. It was unbelievable that my oldest child, whom everyone thought had everything going for her, was dead from a self-inflicted gunshot wound. Nakia left so many hurting people behind; my other two children, Sandra Lynette and Charles Jr. (C.J.), my step-children, Carmen Miekle and Tony Grandberry; and many other family members and friends, too many to name now.

My life had been changed tremendously since Nakia's death. I can't even begin to explain the intense pain I felt at the loss of my daughter. It had been less than a month since her death and I was back at work, yet my emotional state was such that I knew God would have to help me through this. I knew that this time, I would have to depend totally on Him to give me direction. Although my family and church family were very

25

supportive, our pain was tremendous. I knew we needed help. After much prayer, I knew I would have to seek counseling for my family. I was very adamant about having a Christian counselor, so I decided not to go through my job to obtain the services. I started searching, with no success, until I talked to my sister one night. She informed me that she would ask a friend of hers to do the counseling.

My sister's friend's name is Carolyn McKanders. Carolyn declined the request to do the family counseling, and was hesitant about counseling me because she didn't have an office. Nevertheless, after praying, I called Carolyn and she agreed to see me. From the time Carolyn and I met, we knew that God had put us together and that He had something special that He wanted to do for us both.

We had our first meeting on August 11, 1998. This day would prove to be a day that changed both of our lives forever. I prayed throughout the day on August 11th, wondering what Carolyn would be like. What would counseling mean for me? I thought about my pain and wondered if it was worthwhile to go. "Why couldn't I rely on God to heal me? After all, I'm a minister, right? Why would I need a counselor to help me? What could she do that God couldn't do?" I went back and forth all day questioning myself, yet I felt compelled by God to go and meet with Carolyn. I could almost hear God saying to me: "I ordain counselors also to do My work. Let Carolyn help you. I'm sending her to you."

As I drove to the restaurant that evening, I began to feel a sense of peace come over me. I could feel God's love for me, and I somehow knew that help was on the way. Carolyn and I met, we hugged, and I immediately noticed that she was a sincere, kind, caring person. When one is hurting, somehow you are very sensitive to other's reactions to you. I felt Carolyn's compassion toward me. I knew I could be comfortable talking to her.

Carolyn and I sort of just talked for a while, just to get to know each other. I talked about my family and my ministry. Then I began to tell Carolyn about the events leading up to and including July 15th. I told Carolyn how, on the evening of July 14th, Nakia came home and seemed to be very irrational. She insisted that the people at work did not like her and that she had no friends. I asked Nakia if we needed to take her to the hospital? She said, 'no.' After my husband and I talked to her, Nakia seemed to calm down. My husband suggested that he could sleep on the couch so that Nakia could sleep with me. This seemed to please Nakia, so I said okay. Nakia would lie in my arms for over an hour as we laughed and talked. I prayed for her and she turned over and went to sleep.

When I awoke the next morning, everything seemed to be fine. I awakened Nakia before I left for work and asked her if she was okay, and informed her that she could stay home if she wanted. She told me she was fine. I reminded her that in two days, we would be in the Bahamas and that she would have plenty of time to reflect on whether she wanted to keep her job. I hugged her, she told me she loved me, and I left for work. When I arrived at work, I was very uneasy and started calling home. Finally, C. J. answered the phone around 10:30 a.m. but he thought Nakia was gone. I told C. J. to tell her to call me when she came home. Around 12:30 p.m. C. J. called and began to tell me to come home because Nakia was acting foolish and wouldn't get up. He asked me why a gun and bullets were on the floor. I became alarmed and asked him to move her. That's when he started screaming and said there was a hole in her stomach. By the time I got home, the police were at the house. They had C. J. in the police car and refused to let us in the house until the coroner came and removed Nakia's body. Nakia had bled internally; there was no blood anywhere in the room. This partially explained why C. J. thought Nakia was being foolish when she would not respond to his talking to her. C. J. later told us that when he walked into my bedroom that morning, Nakia was on her knees in a praying position like she was every morning. I didn't know that every morning my daughter was praying on the side of my bed. Somehow, Nakia had shot herself and gotten back in a praying position on the side of my bed. Because there was no blood when C. J. entered the room, C. J. thought she was praying.

I could not believe that my child was gone. Parents are not supposed to outlive their children! I shared with Carolyn what occurred over the days preceding the funeral and how I felt during that time. My house was full of people everyday; my church family was very supportive. We were never left alone. My friends from church insisted on staying with us.

I shared with Carolyn how I was compelled to talk to the young people at the funeral, encouraging them to get their lives straight. I gave my message and then directed one of our hearing impaired members in signing a song entitled "We Shall Behold Him." I believe many lives were touched because of the ministry in that song, people were able to release some of their pain. Carolyn and I would have so much to talk about; yet this was a special night; the beginning of many nights to come.

Carolyn and I had been seated in the non-smoking section of the restaurant. Our waitress for the evening was a young lady named Carlo. Carlo proved to be a very special person. She talked to us all evening, sharing about her experiences as a Christian. She told us that we were sitting at the "God table" because the week before, she had talked to two ladies who sat at the same table who were Christians and she told us how they had shared with each other. Carlo would end the evening by affirming for Carolyn that she was doing the right thing in counseling me.

Carlo had no way of knowing that much of Carolyn's and my conversation centered around her ability to do Christian counseling and whether this was really what God wanted her to do. The confirmation came when Carlo told Carolyn and me that God was speaking to her about going into Christian Counseling. She stated her uneasiness about this (the same uneasiness Carolyn had). Then she expressed that God had reassured her that He would help her; all she needed to do was be obedient. Carolyn was flabbergasted; she knew this was a direct Word from the Lord. There was something mysterious about Carlo. We would see her only one more time at our next meeting at the same restaurant. When I tried to contact her, I never got an answer and she was no longer an employee at the restaurant. We often wondered if we were visited by an angel! We left the restaurant that night in awe of God, knowing that He was about to do something special in both of our lives!

Carolyn and I decided that it would be best for us to meet once a week for a while. One thing that really attracted me to Carolyn's style of counseling is that she listened to what God was saying to her. She informed me that she talked to God about what to talk to me about. I knew that Carolyn would understand me when I shared with her what God was revealing to me. I was very comfortable in opening up to her. I never felt the need to hide my true feelings. In fact, I was very expressive, sometimes crying right there in the restaurant.

Right from the beginning it was evident that God's hand was in control of our sessions together. Each time we met, God would have already given Carolyn foreknowledge on what had transpired in me between the times we met. We both were in awe of God and not quite sure of what He was doing. Our sessions were sometimes so long that we would be the last ones remaining in the restaurant.

Time never seemed to be an option with us, because we both knew that God was dealing with both of us. It became obvious to Carolyn and me that God was literally pushing me through this grief process because He had something for me to do. I praise God that Carolyn gave so freely of her time. I realize that God compelled her to assist in my healing process. Carolyn used her professional skills and her spiritual insight to help me through this awful pain I was feeling as I moved through the grief process: denial, depression, anxiety, fear, guilt, anger, and all the other resulting emotions. She helped me to understand what was happening to me emotionally and assured me that I was not losing my mind - I was grieving. I was a normal mother, who was grieving the loss of her child and I had to allow myself to grieve. I had to allow myself to hurt and I did not have to hide that hurt from anyone.

The first couple of sessions Carolyn let me talk out my feelings. I remember telling Carolyn that I felt as if someone had taken my heart out of my chest. The pain was so tremendous and I felt as if no one understood. This emotional pain felt worse than any physical pain I had ever experienced. I was trusting God to get me through this. I now knew what pain, deep emotional pain, felt like. I will never belittle anyone when they tell me they are hurting, no matter how insignificant their issue seems to be. A person's pain is their pain and it must not be taken lightly.

Many times at our sessions, I cried, if I needed to. The tears would come as I talked about Nakia and how I should have known that something was wrong with her. How could I not know? After all, I was her mother. I battled with this guilt, blaming myself for Nakia's death. Carolyn walked me through this process, assuring me that I was not to blame for Nakia killing herself. Nakia was in pain and she wanted to get rid of it. She felt that the only way out of her pain was to kill herself. Carolyn encouraged me to not say that I should have known. I could say that I *wished* I had known, but there was no way I could have known, because Nakia chose not to tell me. It took many sessions for me to finally accept this, even though I still needed to let go of the guilt. Holding on to the guilt would only slow my healing and I wanted to be healed. I finally accepted that no one was to blame, not me, not my husband, not C. J. or Lynette – no one but Nakia. It was her decision. She made it, and she was the one to own it. We could be free to go on with our lives without the guilt that it was our fault.

How could I blame Nakia for this awful thing she did, after all, she was dead? I had to admit that this was my main struggle with letting go of the responsibility – I would have to put the blame where it belonged – on Nakia. Nakia had made a horrible, horrible decision that she could not reverse once it was done. I don't believe that she meant to follow through with it, yet her decision was irreversible and she died. Statistics say that in most suicide attempts/completions people are really crying out for help; they don't really want to die.

Some awesome things began to occur in my sessions with Carolyn that further confirmed that God was in control of our sessions. I am convinced now more than ever that the spirit world is one that we don't understand. At most of our sessions, Carolyn had messages from God for me. Sometimes she would have had a vision in which she saw Nakia, or my mother, and a message was given to me. I don't believe that Nakia can return from the dead. I believe that if God wants to show us His power through a dream or a vision, He can. I don't believe that spirits die. I believe that, for the believer, to be absent from the body is to be present with the Lord. I'm not sure of all that occurred, yet, I believe that God was in control of our meetings and that He used Carolyn to push me through my grief process. Carolyn often told me that my healing progress was phenomenal to her. She stated that for most people who had gone through what I had gone through; it might take years to get to where I was in my healing. I gave all the praise to God for healing me. I knew that God wanted me healed quickly and I would have to cooperate with what He wanted me to do in my life.

As I was able to work through releasing myself from the guilt, there were other areas I needed to work on and God would work through Carolyn to get me through each stage.

God used Carolyn in so many ways in my healing process. Some things were so awesome that we know others would have a hard time believing everything that transpired. On many occasions God told Carolyn what I was dealing with that week or what needed to be dealt with. For instance, I remember very clearly when I was struggling with my fear that my other children, Lynette and C. J., would not survive. I was tormented with the thought that Lynette and C. J. would take their lives or do something so destructive that it would ruin their lives. When I met with Carolyn the week I had all these feelings, she politely informed me that God had specifically told her to tell me that C. J. and Lynette would be ok. She explained how as she prayed for me that week, God had shown her how fearful and doubtful I was. She had vividly felt my pain and fear.

Carolyn proceeded to take out notes she had prepared for that week's session. Little did she know that one of the scriptures she wrote that God gave her to share with me, God had also given me all week long to repeat over and over. "God has not given us the spirit of fear, but of power, of love and of a sound mind" (2 Timothy 1:7)! Carolyn would also assure me that I and my family would be ok - we would not be led by "other voices," my children would know and follow the voice of God. She then shared a scripture that expresses this clearly: "My sheep listen to my voice; I know them and they follow me" (John 10:27). Carolyn would reiterate that my children would be ok, in fact my step children, Carmen and Tony would also be ok, I would be ok and Charles would be ok. Every now and then I still think back on this day, it still gives me strength when I have difficult moments.

We both pray that someone will be blessed as we share how God worked in our lives to push me along in my healing process and how God used Carolyn in this process.

The Mystery of God

I strongly believe that God still speaks to us today if we would only listen. Even in our midst of our pain and sorrow God will hear our cry and answer us. I don't fully understand the mysteries of God and I don't think anyone understands the mind of God for He says, "My thoughts are not your thoughts and My ways are not your ways saith the Lord" Isaiah 55:8. All I know is that God speaks very clearly to me and constantly reassures me of His love for me and His promise never to leave me alone.

Some would think it strange or cruel how God spoke to me even on July 15, 1998 the day of my daughter's death. As I stood outside, waiting for the coroner to come to take my daughter's body from the house God spoke. I could hear the voice of the Lord saying, **"I will take this thing that seems so dark to you and I will change it and use it for My glory."** As I stood for three hours waiting for the coroner to come, God would repeat this message to me several times, I shared it with no one. I would only ponder in my heart what God was saying to me, not fully receiving it because the pain was too great. How could God use the pain I was feeling for His glory? I didn't understand and at the moment I didn't want to understand. All I wanted to know was WHY?

I would ask my whys each night, before the funeral, after everyone was asleep and I was awake. No one knew but God and me how I would awaken and ask God why? Lord, why didn't you intervene and stop my child from killing herself? Why did you allow this to happen? Why so much PAIN! Why MY CHILD, WHY? WHY? WHY?

God would send me a message through a very dear friend of mine. We were sitting in my bedroom one night before the funeral and she looked at me with tears in her eyes and said, "God knows that you are asking Him why. He wants you to know that He will show you why." Needless to say I became overwhelmed and my mind went back to July 15th when God assured me that he would use this dark thing in my life for His glory. What was God doing? How would He use my pain? Was God being fair to me? Why me Lord? What do you want from me? Somehow in the midst of all of these questions, I held on, pondering, believing and trusting God that He would indeed help me get through this and show me what to do with my pain. God has and still is being faithful to His promise to me. How wonderful of God to take time to get messages to little o me, why? Because He loves me!!

Introduction

Carolyn M. McKanders

There are those precious and deeply moving moments in life when we know without a shadow of a doubt that we are being spoken to by God. Such was the time when I met Sandra K. Gordon. Suddenly, major pieces of the last four years of my life fell meaningfully into place. I had completed half the courses toward a doctoral degree in education when I began to feel a strong urge to quit this program and pursue a degree in social work. I knew the chances of my being admitted to a social work program were slim because of my lack of direct social experience. Despite the big obstacle, I was admitted to a masters' degree program in 1994. Fellow students and some of my work colleagues would periodically ask me, "What are you doing in this program?" I would reply, "God put me here," or "This is God's degree." I would come to know the full truth of these statements later. In three years I completed my degree, including an internship, while working full-time and attending to a family. Additionally, I received the Master of Social Work Student of the Year Award. I knew this had to be God and that He had something up, but I didn't know exactly what.

Then, on August 10, 1998, I received a call from a friend asking me to counsel her sister, Sandra Kay, whose daughter had committed suicide about three weeks earlier. I doubted my skill and experience to help during such a tragic life-jarring time. In addition, Sandra stated that she wanted a "Christian" counselor. I felt myself even further less qualified. I retreated and offered to refer her to more qualified counselors. I also explained to Sandra that I didn't even have an office in which to see her. This didn't make any difference to her. In a telephone conversation, she stated very emphatically, "I want you! I trust you to help me." I was unable to reject such trust and agreed to meet Sandra Kay Gordon on the evening of August 11, 1998. What an awesome evening that would be! I knew that evening that both of us had been "set up" by God.

Oh the depth of the riches of the wisdom and knowledge of God!
How unsearchable His judgment, and His paths beyond tracing out.
Romans 11:33

As I drove toward Southfield to meet my counseling client at a restaurant, the idea that I could be of some immediate service caused my emotions to vacillate between anxiety, anticipation, and hopefulness. As I drove, I repeatedly whispered a prayer that I was doing what God wanted and would be successful. I pressed the CD button and listened to my favorite spiritual. As the music played, I let go of the anxiety and allowed myself to be comforted by the lyrics that I heard: "Speak to my heart Holy Spirit, message of love to encourage me..." I drank deeply of these words and each time the song ended, I played it again and again. Still tucked away in my mind, was the thought that I would convince my client to take a referral to another counselor. I held to the hope that in this face-to-face meeting I would persuade her.

I arrived at the restaurant and silently prayed – "Speak to my heart Holy Spirit, message of love..." I stepped into the restaurant anxiously looking for Sandra, having no idea what she looked like. When our eyes met we both knew – "Carolyn?" she said, "Sandra?" I said – we hugged and we were seated.

Sandra began talking about her life and her daughter's suicide immediately. She was open and described that event and its aftermath in detail. We talked for almost half an hour before we noticed that no waiter had come to service our table. I caught the eye of a waitress in another section and beckoned. She quickly came to our table and apologized for the delay, stating that the waiter in our section was newly hired. She introduced herself as "Carlo" and cheerfully offered to take our orders. Carlo's personality was bubbly and she was very talkative – she chattered away nonstop! She stated, "**This** must be the 'God table' because we looked like we liked 'God stuff'." She informed us that she had a good conversation about God with the people who sat in the same booth the week before. We laughed and she finally took our orders. She stated that she had something to tell us later after she took care of customers. Sandra continued to talk in response to my questions. What took place during the next hour and a half was miraculous; it was one of the most spiritually life-changing moments of my life.

Carlo would periodically visit our table to share something about her life experiences. She was serving in another section and not in hearing range of our table, but she would repeat almost verbatim major ideas and explanations that Sandra and I discussed. There was no way that she could have overheard us! Yet with every trip to our table, Carlo would verbally mirror our conversation. For example, Sandra had stated that she knew God was sustaining her. Carlo, seemingly sensing Sandra's distress, stated "Whatever the trouble is in our lives, God will sustain you!"

At first, Sandra and I thought this mirroring was coincidental and humorous, however, after Carlo mirrored our conversation three or four more times, I began to feel that this was a little odd. There was no way Carlo could have overheard us and, yet, her comments were right on target.

Sandra talked of her ministries. She became cheerful as she spoke of one of her favorites, a clown ministry. She described how she combined spiritual teaching with entertainment for children. I found this original and fascinating. Carlo made another visit to our table to tell us that she recently attended a Christian conference and found one aspect of the conference simply delightful – the clown ministry!

When Sandra and I heard these words, it was the last straw. We were dumbfounded. Sandra's eyes filled with tears. I stared. Carlo looked at us apologetically, probably feeling that she said something wrong. She excused herself and hurried away. Sandra and I momentarily sat in silence. Sandra tearfully said, "God is working something here." My rational mind searched frantically for a logical explanation of what was occurring. After all, I was a counselor – reasoning and clear thinking was important to me. I was the one to help make sense of, seemingly, nonsense. I felt somewhat panicked when nothing rational surfaced in my mind. I admitted to Sandra that things were unfolding in quite an unusual way.

We continued our conversation with her explaining her need for a Christian counselor. As I listened intently, I was even more convinced that Sandra needed someone more qualified to counsel her – especially since I didn't consider myself a biblical scholar or as religiously inclined as Sandra's needs appeared to require. I gently stated what I felt. Sandra still insisted that I was who she needed.

Suddenly, a large young man came and sat in the booth directly across from our table. He stated that he was Carlo's husband and had come to pick her up, as it was the end of her shift. He stated that Carlo related to him that she had been talking with us that evening and had hoped that she didn't talk too much or say something offensive. Carlo came over to the table. Her husband launched into this lengthy explanation about how Carlo was a kind person who God had used to save him from the streets. Now, I was really thinking: "What is happening here? Who are all these people?" So now we have Carlo, her husband, Sandra and me in the restaurant.

Sandra told Carlo about her uncanny mirroring of our conversation. She gave her specific examples. Carlo looked stunned for a second and then stated, "God uses me and I feel he wants me to be a Christian counselor." As the words "Christian counselor" echoed in my head, I really thought that this whole evening was some kind of dream. When I focused, Sandra was pointing to me and said to Carlo, "God wants her to do that too!" I sat speechless.

After Carlo and her husband left, Sandra asked emphatically, "Now do you believe that God wants you to counsel me?" From somewhere in the distance, I heard myself say, "Yes, I believe so." We agreed to meet at the same time and place the following week.

I was totally in awe of what had occurred this evening. When we left the restaurant, I sat for a while in my car pondering. I looked at myself in the rearview mirror – still me. On the way home I cried silently, questioning the mysteries of this evening and wondering what God had in store for this counseling relationship.

I settled down for the long ride home, pushed the CD button and was again soothed by the lyrics of my favorite song – "Speak to my heart, Holy Spirit..." The lyrics, however, had a new and much deeper meaning. As I reflect back, clearly, this was only the beginning. God truly spoke to my heart and guided me spiritually to help Sandra heal. I was prepared for each meeting with counseling wisdom, scriptures, prayers, visions, and healing words which were tailored to Sandra's needs. God is truly awesome!

The Mystery of God

One Saturday morning after Sandra and I had met for two counseling sessions, I was praying and meditating as I normally do. I was lying on my back in bed and began to feel somewhat light-headed. Suddenly a vision of a young woman appeared seemingly floating above my bed. The first thing that I did was to reach up and touch my eyes to see if they were opened or closed. I was startled to find my eyes open as I had never experienced envisioning anything with my eyes opened. The vision of the young woman remained. With my heart pounding, I studied the image. The girl looked similar to my daughter, Karla, who was leaving in a week to study abroad in France. I thought to myself, "You are really going to miss her! You are seeing her this way." The vision faded. I was somewhat shaken because I had never done this before. Later that morning, while in the shower, the vision returned. I thought, "Oh, my God, is something going to happen to Karla?" Then I heard a voice very clearly speak, "This is not Karla, this is Nakia." The vision then faded. Troubled and frightened, I hurried from the shower. Throughout the rest of the day the same vision would come and go. I didn't mention these events to my family... I became very reflective. I wondered: "How can this be?" "Am I losing my mind?" I also prayed for guidance from God. "God let me know this is You." "Help me to stay balanced." "Help me to know what to do with this." Even though I remained somewhat anxious, deep inside I felt stillness, a peacefulness that reflected back that it was going to be alright. I didn't trust it fully, but to remain sane it was what I relied on.

My next session with Sandra was on the following Tuesday. Between Saturday and Tuesday the visions came and faded. During our counseling session, I wondered if I would mention what I had experienced to Sandra. Near the end of the session, I casually inquired of Sandra, "Did Nakia have a fair complexion?" Sandra said, "Yes." Then I asked, "Did she have brown hair?" Sandra's eyes narrowed and she curiously replied, "Yes." Then I motioned with my hands on my shoulders and said, "Shoulder length hair." As I motioned toward my eyes, we both said simultaneously, "Big brown eyes." Sandra stared at me and with her eyes filling with tears she said, "Wait a minute. You don't know my baby. You've never seen her. How did you do that?" Then a knowing look came across her face and she looked me in my eyes and said, "You've seen her haven't you?"

I felt dizziness as the reality of my experience set in. Then I burst into tears. I kept repeating, "I don't do this!" To each of my denials, Sandra kept saying, "Yes, you do. You just did it!" We engaged in several rounds of denial and affirmation before Sandra emphatically stated, "Carolyn, it's ok. God is just using you!" She was now consoling me! I calmed a little, but was reeling at the implications of what this might mean. Sandra then began asking me what seemed like a million questions: "What did she look like?" "Was she happy?" "Did she speak?" "What was she wearing?" I was able to describe her smile, her peacefulness and the clothing she wore at her funeral. Sandra smiled and said, "Thank you, God!" I sat teary and dumbfounded. What was God up to?

As I continued to rely on God for guidance and to keep my mind, I learned that this was only the beginning. I began to hear and see Nakia very clearly. I wrote down what I heard. Nearly every week I brought Sandra a message from Nakia. These messages contained events and ideas about Nakia's and Sandra's lives and relationships that I had no way of knowing. My fear gave way to trust. Trust turned into a deep reverence for the expansiveness and awesomeness of God!

I Just Cry

I sit awake at night
Things just don't seem right
Sometimes I laugh, Sometimes I smile
But most times, I just cry, cry, cry.
Why Lord, Why? is a question I often ask
"My child, My child, I've put you in a special class."
But it's too hard Lord, I'll never pass
Then he says, "My child, my child, you of little faith,
I've taught you better, Now get up and do as I saith"
I'll try Lord, I'll try, but most times, I just cry, cry, cry.
He says, "Dry your eyes,
And don't you believe that devil's lies,"
But Lord, he's so sneaky, conniving, and sly
Well, what are you going to do?
Are you going to lie, lie down as his doormat?,
Or are you going to stand, stand, as my elect
And proclaim "Those are lies, but I've got the facts."
Okay Lord, no longer will I just cry, cry, cry
But I will realize that I am in a special class
And I am determined to pass, pass, pass.
I will dry my eyes
And I will not bow down to the devil's lies
No longer will I just cry, cry, cry
But I will rise to the challenge
Yes, I will Rise, Rise, Rise!

Written by Madelyn McCargo
August, 1998

Chapter One

"It Hurts!"

"Hear my cry, O God; attend unto my prayer. From the ends of the earth will I Cry unto thee, when my heart is overwhelmed: lead me to the rock that is higher than I."

Psalms 61: 1 – 2

I talked a little in the introduction about the intense emotional pain I was in after my daughter killed herself. I believe it warrants more discussion, because emotional pain is what caused my daughter to take her life. No one knows the depths of another person's pain, especially if you have never experienced serious emotional pain yourself. For the first time in my life, I understood what someone meant when they said they were hurting. I was hurting so badly and I didn't know how to stop the hurt. I knew to pray and trust that God would help me, yet, this pain was one I had never experienced before. I remember Carolyn asking me where it hurt. All I knew was that my entire insides were racked with emotional pain and I felt that no one understood. Despite all the enormous support I had from my family and church family, I still felt so very alone in my pain. My husband and my other children were indeed hurting, but for me, losing my child, who I had carried in my womb for nine months, I was devastated. I couldn't bear not seeing her anymore, yet, I knew that was indeed the case; that on this side of eternity, I would never see my Nakia again.

Although I knew and believed that I would see Nakia in heaven, not being able to see her physically here on earth hurt so badly. I could recall many scriptures that reassured me that I would see her again, such as: "To be absent from the body is to be present with the Lord," and scriptures about the resurrection of the body in the last days. I held on to this and trusted God, yet, the moments came when my pain was so intense that it nearly consumed me. I can say that it is only by God's grace that I was able to make it through. I realized that God had greater plans for me. I never had suicidal thoughts, but I understood how someone could have those thoughts. When the pain is so intense, all you want to do is to end the pain and, at times, this means by any means necessary, even if that means killing yourself. God did not allow me to get this far in my pain. God always provided the help that I needed each time by sending a message my way or sending someone who ministered to me. There are certain areas that seemed to cause more pain than others, such as the reality of not seeing Nakia and making it through anniversaries, holidays, and birthdays. I will discuss each of these, briefly.

My heart ached each day as I came into the house and I knew Nakia wasn't home. I would pass her room, peeking in, somehow thinking I would see her. Perhaps I had only had a terrible nightmare and I would awaken, and Nakia would be home soon. I could smell her scent in her room and soon this became unbearable to me. It didn't matter if I opened the windows or used air fresheners, I could still smell her body scent. I decided to close her bedroom door. For weeks I would not enter her room. Even if others opened the door, I would go behind and close it. I could not even think about giving her clothes away. Everything remained the same in her room, just the way she left it. Whenever my husband, Charles, would ask me when was I going to clear out her room, I would tell him, I wasn't ready yet. I remember coming home from a weekend retreat when my daughter, Lynette, informed me that my husband had gotten rid of Nakia's clothes. I was so upset with Charles that the next morning, when I went into her room and indeed found out that her belongings had been removed, I was unable to go to work. I laid in the bed and cried for hours. Charles came home and brought the clothes back into the house. He later told me that when he removed the clothes from the house, he was led to take them to the garage and not the Salvation Army, like he had planned. When he saw the results of my reaction to the clothes, he knew why he was unable to take the clothes to the Salvation Army. For me, removing the clothes somehow meant departing from Nakia, and I couldn't stand the thought of doing that. I knew, however, that the clothes were just that, clothes. I knew that Lynette and I would soon have to decide what to do with the clothes and I also knew that there was no rush on the time; when we were both ready, we could deal with what to do with Nakia's clothes.

Again, Carolyn walked me through the pain. She assured me that I was ok and that it was normal for me to have this type of reaction. It was all a part of the grieving process. Getting rid of Nakia's clothes meant separating with Nakia, and that was too painful to do now. Carolyn also helped me to understand that my husband was also dealing with grief. Perhaps, looking at her room and her clothes was just too painful for him. She explained to me that Charles also had to work out his own grief, his way. I ended up compromising with Charles; the clothes were taken out of Nakia's room and placed in the basement. Lynette and I would go through them when we were ready.

I wondered why my pain was so intense. I struggled with all of this, because after all, aren't ministers supposed to be in control of their feelings? Going to church was difficult sometimes, because Nakia's friends were constant reminders to me of Nakia. Just looking at them caused me to burst into tears. I found myself avoiding them or cutting my conversations short with them; anything that would get me out of their presence.

I had mixed emotions about staying in my own bedroom. It was in my room that Nakia had killed herself. My husband and I slept in there from the first night, yet, I had difficulty sleeping in the room if my husband was not home. I avoided going into the room until he came home. In my mind, I kept trying to envision why she did that in my room. I slept more comfortably if my husband was in bed with me; the room at times being more of a comfort than a discomfort. Sometimes I could feel the presence of Nakia sleeping next to me, awakening at times to tell my husband to move over, only to find out he was not in the bed!

After about six months, we made a decision to put our house up for sale. We thought it would be better for all of us to move, change the environment and get on with our lives. We came very close to selling the house. I vividly remember the day the realtor told me she thought she had sold the house; I cried all morning and ended up calling Carolyn from work. Carolyn walked me through my thoughts and feelings, which revealed that I had convinced myself that leaving the house would mean leaving Nakia and all memories of her behind. I worked through this and months later, although we decided not to sell the house, I knew I would be fine if and when we decided to sell it.

I never really understood the impact that anniversaries, holidays and birthdays had on people who were grieving the loss of their loved one, until now. After the death of my mother (Selma Murphy), I experienced some pain when the holidays came, but nothing like this. I remember in September of 1998 when Carolyn tried to prepare me for how I might be feeling on Nakia's birthday (October 15th). She encouraged me to make sure that I had planned my day well and to plan something for the family to do to commemorate Nakia. I soon learned that, with me, my pain seemed to come days before the actual meaningful day (birthday, holiday or anniversary of death). The anticipation of the actual day probably caused me to experience the pain prior to the actual day.

Although I know of others who are incapacitated when these special days come around (usually staying in bed), that has not been the answer for me. I seem to have to work through my grief. Staying in the bed is not good for me. I know this, so I challenge myself to get up and get moving, doing something. I am also a talker and I have no hesitation in calling someone and telling them I'm hurting and I need to talk. Further, in my hardest moments, God has pushed me through my pain, by compelling me to minister to others.

I know that God has done some special things for me to help me get through these *special days*. I'll just list a few of them. On December 30, 1998 (This would have been mother's

74th birthday), I preached my initial sermon at Greater New Mt. Moriah Baptist church and received my license to preach. On July 15, 1999 (Anniversary of Nakia's death), I was busy teaching a class for the Michigan Progressive Baptist Convention. On October 15, 1999 (This was Nakia's 25th birthday), I preached my very first eulogy for one of the members at our church. As I write, things continue to happen on these special days. On July 15, 2000, I was busy preparing for a class I would teach at Greater Southern Baptist Church. On October 15, 2000, I preached at the 7:45 a.m. service at our church for Women's Day. I have come to realize that this is all very therapeutic for me. I thank God for how He has chosen to use me and help me get through my grief. I've learned to not ask God why so much pain, but to ask Him what He wants me to do with this pain. Each time I ask this question, He provides someone for me to minister to. Each day I'm learning that God does not want me to stay in my pain; He wants me to get through it, and the best way for me to get through it, is by helping others – To God be the Glory!

Reflections from Carolyn

"It Hurts!"

The pain that Sandra felt was deep and so tangible. I wondered if I could actually help alleviate the pain and move her toward healing. Then I realized that I had to do nothing and, of myself, I could do nothing. God had brought us together and it was He who would deliver Sandra from the depths of despair and into the light of healing and peace. I needed only to be a conduit for God's love, mercy, compassion and wisdom. I decided to listen attentively to God's directions. God helped me to use my experience, knowledge, and skill in just the right way to help Sandra. He alone knew exactly what Sandra was feeling and exactly where it hurt. My job was to tune into the voice of God so that His will would be done in both of us. Therefore, my constant prayer became, "Holy Spirit I surrender to the will of God; open me to His divine wisdom; may I say what He wants me to say, ask what He wants me to ask, hear what He wants me to hear, do what He wants me to do and feel what He wants me to feel in each moment."

Miraculously, God mixed just the right amount of counseling wisdom and scriptural wisdom to help Sandra understand her pain and know very deeply that He was walking this very difficult walk with her. God gave me the appropriate psychological terminology in a way that made Sandra comfortable with her pain – to let Sandra know that the pain she was feeling was absolutely normal and a part of the grieving and healing process. Also, Sandra understood that each pain or painful experience moved her to the peace she so greatly desired. She understood that feeling and expressing the pain was necessary to heal. Sandra was extraordinary in staying with her pain, feeling it very deeply and expressing it through crying and talking honestly about her feelings.

Many people are afraid of the pain and run from it or suppress it, hoping that by not paying attention to it that it will somehow disappear. I explained to Sandra that suppressing the pain was one of the worst things she could do, because it doesn't go away, it just disguises itself as physical aches and pains, mood swings, compulsive behaviors, lack of energy, sleeplessness, fear, anxiety, and other maladaptive behaviors. It is best to deal with the pain in the moment, wading into it, expressing it with someone you trust. At times, the intensity of Sandra's pain made her feel as if she would be drowned by it, yet, she persevered. Sandra knew how to reach out to God and to others, during these critical periods. She wasn't ashamed or afraid to cry out to God for help and, time after time, miraculously God would send her the right message through just the right person at just the right moment to keep her afloat, soothing the agony of the loss of her daughter. She and I both marveled at the goodness of God. Sandra also, reached out often to friends and her pastor. She allowed herself to be nurtured by acts of kindness and compassionate conversation.

Sandra's faith and gratitude, also, provided a healing balm to her pain. She stated during our first meeting, that God was sustaining her and that she had total faith that while the lost of her daughter hurt tremendously, He was still in charge. She believed that there was divine order and that God had something important for her to do. I was stunned at this level of faith from someone whose daughter had committed suicide, just a few weeks earlier. Suicide survivors are supposed to have what is called "complicated grief" because of the complexity of the situation around which the death occurs. The ways in which Sandra was embracing her pain were amazing and encouraging for her sanity and healing. Her consistent and sincere expressions of thanks, helped Sandra to be very conscious of her progress, which gave her hope and, thus, reduced her pain. Further, gratitude is healing. It makes us feel connected – it connects us to God, to our spirit and the spirit of others. We feel that we are not alone and this is healing.

God provided me with scriptures for Sandra, even though I was in no way a bible scholar. I was directed to a passage of scripture, which fit so well with what she was feeling. For example, Proverbs 3:5-6 *"Trust in the Lord with all thine heart and lean not to thine own understanding. In all thy ways acknowledge him and he will direct thy path."* Two things seemed to lift Sandra's spirit – the fact that God knew exactly what she was feeling and that He directed me to the scripture that would express so clearly His love for her and His desire to squelch the sting of her pain.

My Reflections

"It Hurts!"

_____

_____

_____

_____

_____

_____

_____

_____

_____

_____

_____

_____

_____

_____

Chapter Two

"I'm Not Guilty!"

"There is therefore now no condemnation to them which are in Christ Jesus, who walk not after the flesh but after the Spirit."   Romans: 8:1

The issue most prevalent in my life that I knew I needed to confront were my feelings of guilt concerning my daughter's suicide. This issue was probably the hardest issue Carolyn had to help me work through. It seemed like we would take a step forward in working through the guilt, only for me to move backward, again. I had trouble letting go of the guilt feelings. Carolyn, again, was very patient with me and would take me slowly through. She quietly listened to me and let me talk about my feelings of guilt. I was able to express to her exactly how I felt after Nakia's suicide.

For months after Nakia's suicide, I exhibited all the signs of someone who was feeling guilty. I felt tremendous despair and shame. I felt inadequate and unfit to be a mother and I blamed myself for my daughter's death. I accused myself of being a failure as a mother, as a wife, and as a youth leader in my church. I could not forgive myself. It didn't matter what Carolyn said to me to try to get me through this, as I kept badgering myself. I found myself guilty of not being able to save my daughter. It was all my fault.

I had so many irrational beliefs going through my mind. The one that probably surfaced the most was that I failed Nakia. I had not been a good mother to her; if I had, she would not have taken her life. I insisted that I could have done more to be there for Nakia. I must have done something wrong as a mother. I felt so helpless and worthless. My firstborn child was gone from a self-inflicted gunshot wound and I could not fix this. How could I have been so blind to have not seen the trouble/pain my daughter must have been in? Why didn't I see the signs? What was wrong with me? How could I have failed my daughter this way? How she must have felt so all alone - that no one cared - not even me, her mother. I thought that Nakia and I had a good relationship and that I had been a pretty good mother to my children. Boy, was I wrong – I thought.

I had always tried to be a good mother. I expected that of myself. I thought I had done pretty well, until now. Now, I was condemning the offender and the offender was me! The utter despair and shame I felt. I failed everyone, including myself. How could I continue to be a youth leader at my church after this? My pastor had asked me to be the Director of Youth Ministries. I wasn't sure if I could accept this position, not after this. How could I work with other youth and I couldn't save my own child? No one would want me as a youth leader anymore, not even me. Who would want me to work with their children? For over 20 years, I had been a youth worker, and now my own child had taken her life. How could I even hold my head up now?

I put myself on trial, tried myself, served as my own jury and found myself guilty on all counts: not being a good mother, not being there for Nakia, not being fit to be a youth worker or a minister. There was no need for others to convict me; I had convicted myself! God and others certainly would have no use for me, not after what I had done. My daughter killed herself, and it was my entire fault. I may as well had shot her myself. She wasn't to blame, it was me!

These now seemingly irrational thoughts were real at the time. It would take me months to work through this. Carolyn helped me sort through the feelings of guilt. She helped me to understand that I could not take the blame for Nakia's suicide. Nakia had made a very bad mistake that could not be corrected; yet, it was her decision. I did not see the signs because Nakia chose, for the most part, to hide them from everyone. Carolyn helped me to understand the importance of saying, "I *wish* I had known" instead of "I should have known." I didn't know because Nakia chose not tell anyone about her pain and her plan to take her life.

Was God somehow showing me that, yes, I am a minister, but I am also human and humans do have struggles that need to be worked through?

Aside from all this guilt, I further beat up on myself for feeling guilty. As a minister, I should know better than to allow myself to feel the pain and guilt I felt. I prayed and prayed and prayed, yet, the guilt feelings did not leave. Why was I having so much trouble with this? Why won't these feelings go away once and for all? I knew how to pray, what scriptures to use to console myself, yet, I was still struggling. Why? Was God somehow showing me that, yes, I am a minister, but I am also human and humans do have struggles that need to be worked through? With God's help and Carolyn's counseling, I slowly began to come around and really deal with this issue of guilt.

Carolyn's counseling helped me to take a good look at how I had tried to raise my children and assured me that while I couldn't do everything perfectly, I was a good mother. We carefully explored my past intentions, feelings and actions. She helped me to accept that my own children do love and admire me. I had not been a failure, as I thought; even Nakia loved me. God spoke through Carolyn on many occasions: at times, through visions of Nakia and my mom; other times, direct words from the Lord. We both were in awe at first of how God was using her, but soon we realized that we were both on a path. God was using Carolyn to heal me. God wanted me healed in all areas, because He had work for me to do.

Carolyn also helped me to understand that my role as a youth leader had been a successful one. The youth at church and in the neighborhood respect and love me. After much prayer, I decided to tell Pastor Flowers I would assume the position as Director of Youth Ministries. With God's help, I could help other youth. The young people seemed to be drawn to me. I think they come because they know that I won't condemn or judge them. I try to show them love and give them hope instead of despair. I sometimes still struggle with releasing these guilty feelings, yet God continuously shows His unconditional love for me.

Although it is over ten years that Nakia has been gone, I realize that I still have my moments when I struggle with my feelings of guilt. Just the other Sunday, a young person came to the church in despair, searching for me. He found me and I was able to help him. The next day, I found myself slipping into depression. Instead of rejoicing because I had helped to save another life, I found myself wondering why I hadn't saved my Nakia.

As I write this, I realize that I sometimes still struggle with my own feelings of self-worth. I realize now that my sense of self-worth can only be assured by God's unconditional gift of love for me. I also know that there is no condemnation for those who are in Christ Jesus (Romans 8:1). I know that I have tried to do the best I can as a mother, wife and youth leader. I know that I have tried to follow Proverbs 22:6, "Train up a child in the way he should go and when he is old he will not depart from it."

I know and understand that I was not a perfect mother. I've made plenty of mistakes along the way and God has forgiven me. I need to forgive myself. I also must understand that none of these mistakes were the cause of Nakia's death. It was not my fault. I know that my daughter knew the Lord and I have the assurance that she is now with the Lord in heaven. Nakia accepted Christ at the age of 6 and had a passionate love for the Lord. I find my peace in knowing that I did indeed raise her right – she did know Christ. Whatever went so wrong that day on July 15, 1998, only God knows; but I have to understand and know that it is not my fault. I find my peace in helping others and knowing that I will one day see Nakia again!

Reflections from Carolyn

"I'm Not Guilty"

The presumption of guilt directed at suicide survivors by society is devastating; yet, unfortunately, survivors are often their own severest judges. Suicide survivors often torment themselves asking such questions as: Why didn't I see that my loved one was depressed? Why didn't I force her to get help? Why didn't I return his last phone call? Why did I say such terrible things to him during that last argument? The decision to commit suicide creates a sense of utter helplessness for those left behind. In order to maintain a sense of control, they often blame the death of their loved ones on actions they took or omissions they made, (Carl Fine, *No Time to Say Goodbye*).

Thus, most survivors of suicide labor under a thick fog of guilt. Just as they seem to make a clearing in the fog, a memory, a comment, an emotion, a situation, or someone triggers self – incriminating thoughts and the shroud of guilt returns. Survivors' feelings are deep, often silent and persistent. Feelings of guilt resulting from the suicide of one's child seem to be *the* most difficult and pernicious emotion that survivors must confront. In Sandra's case, she tore into herself time and time again. She made all kinds of accusations against herself. She would verbalize: "As a mother, how could I miss her signs of distress?" "Why was my love not enough?" "We talked about everything and I thought she was fine." "What do my other children think of me?" "What did Nakia think of me?" "I'm such a failure as a mother!" On and on went her struggle with only very brief periods of reprieve. Ultimately, she believed that she, and she alone, should have been able to save her child and that she must have done something very painful. In addition, she felt that others must be judging her, too. How could she continue her church responsibilities? Surely, people were thinking that she wasn't a good mother and couldn't possibly be qualified to minister to others, especially to children. Though Sandra could talk through the irrationality of many of the allegations, criminations, and faulty beliefs, and many times could not find the supporting evidence to convict herself, she still found it extremely difficult to begin to let go of the feelings of guilt.

As her counselor, while I knew that all Sandra's feelings and struggles were normal, I pondered long and hard about these gripping feelings of guilt. I knew that as painful as it was, survivors consistently replay mental tapes trying to reconstruct the factors that may have influenced their loved ones' decision to complete suicide. They comb and sieve through minute details - hanging onto words, phrases, a certain look or expression, arguments, conversation, interactions, relationships, last events, last steps, mental pictures of the suicide act, and the aftermath - looking for an answer. This search rarely leads to a satisfying answer to justify the act and put a final peaceful closure to the event. In this context, the guilt continues to surface as the survivor is left with feelings of inadequacy, helplessness, and deep feelings of loneliness. The "investigations" yield nothing lastingly fruitful and the survivor contends, "It must be me!" This is played out over and over which leads to exhaustion, confusion, and despair. Because the solution to the puzzle of suicide lies exclusively with the people who have killed themselves, often survivors' rational explanations and logical conclusions are of little comfort to survivors. (Carla Fine, *No Time to Say Goodbye*).

Another catch-22 issue is that guilt and blame provide a way for the survivors to connect to the experience of their loved one's death. Survivors feel anger and helplessness for being left out of the loved ones' decision to end his/her life. Though painful, the guilt and self-crimination can offer a context for the survivor's mourning and a means to be included in the death choice of the loved one. The survivors, however, are caught in an unproductive cycle of empty detachment and being attached to their loved ones by guilt and blame. Because of the complexity and deep emotions involved in guilt, it takes self-awareness, patience, spiritual connections, education, dialogue in a psychologically – safe environment, encouragement, life-affirming self-talk and conscious use of strategies to combat irrational self-talk.

Some strategies that Sandra used, with my encouragement, were: prayer and scriptures which affirmed her innocence; connecting with positive friends; journaling about feelings and situations which triggered guilt; education about the process of grieving; talking with spiritual colleagues and her pastor; talking with her spouse about his feelings and expressing hers; expressing her feelings in writing and verbally to her deceased daughter, including asking her to forgive her for anything she may have done or not done; being honest in counseling about her guilt; taking a break from grieving; praising herself for all the wonderful things she had done and was continuing to do in her life; writing, posting and saying positive affirmations/statements of the truth, especially when the irrational self-talk popped in her head; nurturing herself; and becoming involved in suicide prevention work.

A significant turning point in the healing of Sandra's feelings of guilt came when she and I looked realistically at her life with Nakia and as a mother. I gave Sandra the much-needed opportunity to talk about those things she could have done better. It was important for her to say that she wasn't perfect and that she indeed was human and regretted some parenting decisions. This is an important step because it gives the survivor a chance to voice anything hidden in their mind that they feel too ashamed or afraid to discuss. This kind of dialogue needs to occur in an accepting, nonjudgmental setting. It provides a context for asking God, the deceased loved one, and ones-self for forgiveness. Finally, saying the unthinkable, or seemingly unspeakable, provides a pathway for releasing much of the shame and self-crimination because the survivor can now believe that forgiveness is based on the truth...a realistic examination of their life.

It was important for her to say that she wasn't perfect and that she indeed was human and regretted some parenting decisions.

My Reflections

"I'm Not Guilty!"

_____

_____

_____

_____

_____

_____

_____

_____

_____

_____

_____

_____

_____

_____

_____

_____

_____

I Want a Sign

I'm confused Lord, And I don't know why
I just sit back and let out a great big sigh
It's so gloomy, can't you just give me a little relief
My heart aches and there's oh so much grief
I want to cry, but I don't because on you I rely
I want a sign Lord, won't you please hear my cry.
Perhaps your bright sunshine
Or even turning water into wine
Or even in front of my enemies making me dine
I call you sometimes on your direct line
I know you get tired of me 'cause I just whine, whine, whine.
But please Lord, please, I just want a little sign.
Lord, I just want a little peace
Because you see Lord, between you and me I'm a little angry
You told me to lay out my fleece
So please Lord just let it be
I want a sign don't you see.
While your plea is a its peek,
Be quiet and let me speak
I know that you are restless
But in me is where rest is
So come unto me
And there your sign will be.

Written by: Madelyn McCargo
August, 1998

Chapter Three

"I'm Mad!"

"In Your anger do not sin: Do not let the sun go down while you are still angry, and do not give the devil a foothold."   *Ephesians 4: 26 -27*

Perhaps the hardest part for me to express as I traveled through this grief process, was my anger. Being a minister, I don't know if I felt that I needed to control my anger, but I would not allow myself to be angry. Carolyn periodically asked me about my anger. Each time I would tell her, no – that I wasn't angry.

Although the gun that Nakia shot herself with was my husband's, I was not angry with him. I did not blame him, not once. I seemed to have an abundance of compassion for him instead of anger. I saw no reason to be angry with Lynette or C. J. Again, I felt compassion instead of anger. I wanted them all to be ok and, therefore, there was no room for me to be angry with them. I could not allow myself to be angry with God; after all, God is God and what right did I have to be angry with Him? Although, I knew that God could have intercepted Nakia's thoughts, obviously, He chose not to. God is sovereign; He can do what He wants to when He wants to, how He wants to. I certainly could not allow myself to be angry with Nakia because she's my daughter and is now dead; I couldn't dare be angry with her for taking her life.

Carolyn would have me revisit anger periodically during our sessions. In January of 1999, something happened on my job that caused me to direct my anger at God. I met a co-worker who was returning from maternity leave. This may not seem like a big deal, except for the fact that she looked just like my daughter, Nakia. I was actually looking for someone else when I happened to walk over to her area and I saw someone sitting in a cube that looked just like my daughter. I looked at her; she looked at me and said, "Hi, it's so good to see you again." I was in shock. I didn't recall ever meeting her, but she said she remembered me from a team meeting we had the previous year. She purposely (it seemed), continued to talk to me, periodically holding my hand. When we finally finished talking, I started to walk away, but turned to her and told her how much she looked like my daughter, Nakia. Monique's response surprised me. She said: "I know." I must have looked absolutely petrified. She took my hand and told me that on the day of the funeral when the other co-workers whom I had worked with for years returned to the office from the funeral, they showed her the obituary. She looked at Nakia's picture and thought – oh my God, she looks like me. As soon as I walked away from Monique, I fell into the arms of my friend Mary, crying and asking her what was God doing to me. Why was He allowing this to happen? Why was there a girl on my job that I have to look at almost every day, who looks like my daughter? I was mad at God. I thought He was being very cruel to me. Mary calmed me down and let me talk for awhile until I was able to return to my seat. I got myself together and called

Carolyn. She walked me through some things. We explored how I could perceive all this and what I did think God was saying to me. I told Carolyn that I thought God probably wanted me to be comforted, because I missed Nakia so. The very next day, Monique came over to me and informed me that this was not supposed to be hard for me. She knew that she was supposed to be a comfort to me. After the initial shock of it all, Monique turned out to be a blessing to me. She was only on the job for a few months, but she continues to be a very important part of my life. It's almost as if God allowed her to stay there just long enough to accomplish what was needed (to help me), and then she moved on to other things. Monique and I have stayed in contact with each other. It seems like she always shows up or calls when I am having a difficult time about Nakia. She is like a daughter to me and has asked me to be godmother to her third child she will soon have. I have also been able to mentor her in regard to her call into ministry. She has recently accepted her call into the preaching ministry and has received her license to preach.

Carolyn began to strongly encourage me to deal with my anger with Nakia. She felt it was important for me to be able to express any anger that I could be harboring in order to proceed in my healing process. She gave me assignments – to write God a letter and to write Nakia, but I could not do them.

Finally, on the evening of March 4, 1999 (my 26th wedding anniversary), as I waited to board a plane to Phoenix, Arizona to attend a Women's Conference, the intensity of my pain caused me to pull out a pad and pen and begin to write. I remember starting my letter by saying to God: "Alright, alright!!" If this is what you want from me, I'll write." (Sounds like I was a little angry with God, huh?). I wrote a letter to Nakia, expressing my anger at her shooting herself. On the flight I continued to write and cry for two hours. No one was aware of my tears; both the men I sat between on the flight were fast asleep!

I wanted Nakia to know how hurt I was and how I wished she had come to me. I could have gotten her help, if she only had told me what was going on with her. I thought we talked about everything, but obviously we didn't. I wanted Nakia to realize that so many people loved her. She should have thought of how we would feel if she killed herself. She should not have done this horrible thing. C. J., Lynette, Carmen, and Tony (her siblings) were all hurting so deeply, and it was all her fault. I wanted to yell and scream right there on the plane, but all I could do was quietly cry and continue to write. I somehow knew that I was now progressing through another part of the grief process. I had desperately needed to express this anger. When I met Carolyn, she assured me that this was a good thing. It is ok for me to be angry with Nakia. Yes, she was my daughter and she did something I disapproved of. If she was living and had done something I didn't approve of, I would have expressed my anger; therefore, even in her death it is ok for me to be mad at her. It was time for me to deal with the anger and be able to express it. I was so angry with Nakia. I knew God was helping me get through this. He had given me Carolyn as a counselor and was constantly ministering to me. I knew I would be ok.

If she was living and had done something I didn't approve of, I would have expressed my anger; therefore, even in her death it is ok for me to be mad at her.

The intensity of my anger would come when I thought about the rest of my family: her dad, Charles, and her siblings. I especially could not understand how she could have done this to her sister, Lynette. Lynette was in so much pain from losing her sister. She refused further counseling and refused to talk about Nakia. Lynette and Nakia were 22 months apart, so they had been rather close. They did a lot of things together, wore each other's clothes, and frequently hung out together. Other than the usual sibling rivalry, they got along well and I knew that Nakia was more than a sister to Lynette; she was her friend. I could not talk Lynette into getting help and this frustrated me and made me even angrier at Nakia.

Many of Nakia's friends, and some of her cousins, were having a very difficult time coping with her death. Some of them desperately needed counseling, but they refused to go. They didn't want any one to think they were crazy. I tried to convince them that it's alright to go to counseling; God ordains counselors. After all, I'm a minister and I needed counseling. They still would not go — so Carolyn equipped me to be able to talk to them and measure if they were in a crisis state. On two occasions, I had to insist on someone getting help because they had become suicidal themselves. Nakia's death had changed the lives of so many people. I was mad with her for not thinking this through, causing so much pain and turmoil in her friends' lives.

It is hard for me to think about what C. J. must have been going through. He's the one who found Nakia. To find his sister dead in his mother's room must be so devastating to him. It's hard for me to even imagine how he must feel sometimes. I become angry with Nakia for how she has shattered our lives. I wonder sometimes what C. J. is thinking, how all this has affected him and will he be able to get his life together. I see him sometimes acting out his anger and grief and I become frustrated because I don't know what to do for him.

Carmen and Tony, although they are not my biological children, I love them as if they were mine. They loved Nakia so much and Charles and I worked so hard at letting them know that they are a part of the family. They were not to consider themselves half sisters and brothers, but simply sisters and brothers, and were to treat each other as such. Carmen had been away from us a while and only recently had started coming around us more often. She and Nakia had bonded, as sisters should. How could Nakia do this to her, just when she was starting to love us again? Tony was so hurt and did not know what to do. I remember Tony telling me that he did not know if he could go on. I remember, before the funeral, that I had to talk to him and share with him the importance of holding on and allowing God to help him get through this. Again, I fought off the thoughts of how could Nakia do this to her sisters and brothers. I pray a lot for them; that they will seek a closer relationship with God. I can only trust that God is taking care of Lynette, C. J. , Carmen and Tony, and that He will show Charles and me what to do for them. He will send the help that is needed. I must believe and trust that to be the truth.

In October of 1999, I once again had to briefly acknowledge my anger to God. This time, I was so overwhelmed, yet, compelled to do something that others would have thought probably to be too much to ask someone who was still grieving. I was asked to do the eulogy at a funeral for the grandmother of Tracy (Nakia's friend), who just happened to have also been a very good friend of my mother's. I hadn't done a eulogy yet! This would be my first. I was to do this eulogy on October 15, 1999, which would have been Nakia's 25th birthday! With my husband and my Pastor at the funeral with me, I preached the eulogy that morning. That evening we celebrated Kim's birthday (our Pastor's wife). What was God teaching me? Perhaps to take the focus off myself and concentrate on helping others. I experienced a brief moment of anger at God because I didn't understand what He was trying to do for me. Now, I understand and am overwhelmed with His love for me. Usually when any anniversary day comes – the anniversary of Nakia's death, her birthday, etc. – I have something to do to keep me busy and to take the focus off my pain and myself.

I've learned that it is ok to be angry with Nakia because it's all a part of the grieving process. I am able to express my anger more freely now. Talking about Nakia and my anger helps me tremendously. I believe it keeps me from getting stuck in my anger. By expressing it, I'm able to release the anger and go on doing the things I need to do.

Reflections from Carolyn

"I'm Mad"

Anger is a very natural emotion, one that is needed to let ourselves and others know when things are not 'ok' with us. However, most of us have been taught as children that anger is bad, very bad and definitely not appropriate to express. As a result, as adults, we believe that mature "good" people don't get mad. Right? Wrong! Emotionally mature people know how to recognize and express their anger. Repressed anger becomes something very unnatural - debilitating rage and boiling resentment. Rage and resentment are destructive, both to the person harboring them and to those at which they are openly and passively directed. The intensity of theses emotions is often frightening and difficult to express. Rage can also intensify guilt and destroy relationships. In order to be healthy, whole and heal, we must learn to accept our anger as a natural part of ourselves and learn positive, life-affirming ways to express it. Anger can be our friend and ally on the grieving journey. In fact, acknowledging and releasing anger, rage and resentment is a primary goal in healing.

...acknowledging and releasing anger, rage and resentment is a primary goal in healing.

As a counselor, I knew how important it was for Sandra to be angry. I also knew how difficult it was to allow oneself to feel this very powerful emotion in the context of grief. It takes time, but anger does surface. Sandra's initial denial of anger was not troublesome in this light. I knew she wasn't ready and it was important for her to move at her own pace and in her own way. However, I kept a watchful eye, monitoring her progress. As she worked through other issues and thawed emotionally, anger finally surfaced. She was surprised at the quantity and depth of her anger. It was initially directed at God and, soon after, at Nakia for taking her life and causing so much pain. This is quite normal. She blamed God for not intervening – after all He is all knowing and all powerful and how could he allow such a horrible thing? She really let Him have it! I was really relieved at her full expression of anger, rage and resentment. Her written letter to God allowed her to say all that she needed to say with privacy. Sometimes, we can write down what we dare not express aloud. Also, writing it is less frightening because once the anger gate opens, the emotions just flood through, which can be extremely overwhelming. It often allows an individual a way to safely find their voice after the feelings surface. Sandra kept her letters and found it helpful to later reread them as a testimony to her progress through grief.

Sandra also expressed her anger toward God verbally. In a break-through session, she admitted how angry she was with God. I assured her that her anger was normal and that she needed to feel what she was feeling and to express it. It was also important for her to know that this expression was key to her healing. Once she fully understood the importance of anger, knew it was quite "OK" to be angry and recognized her own rage (and vented it), she dealt with it openly and learned productive ways to handle and release it. She felt lighter and more free. The surfacing of anger shows that the person in grief is coming out from the depths of depression and can signal the beginning of the healthy expression of feelings again, without debilitating fear.

Expression of anger toward the deceased is more complex and difficult. With the onset of anger toward the deceased, comes a rush of other emotions such as fear, resentment, shame and, the biggie, guilt. The survivor is fearful of both the intensity of the anger and for having these thoughts and feelings toward the deceased. They fear that something must be wrong with them for being angry. Faulty thoughts such as the following are common: "After all, how could I be so enraged at her (the deceased), she was in so much pain that she took her life." "She was the one hurting and now she's dead." "She's been hurt enough without my being angry with her." "Anyway, I should have been able to save her." "It's all my fault."

Nevertheless, the angry feelings keep coming and get stronger. While these feelings are to be expected, this can be scary and needs to be talked about with a caring, competent person. Expression may create tension, putting the griever in a double bind. While holding these feelings inside intensifies the fear and prevents healing, expressing the resentment and anger at the deceased might also trigger intense feelings of shame and guilt. There are feelings of guilt for being angry at the "helpless" deceased person and the gnawing shame and guilt of feeling responsible for the death or for not being able or good enough, somehow, to prevent the death.

Sandra needed a lot of assurance that anger, even rage, are OK to have toward Nakia. It was difficult, but she expressed her anger by writing and speaking it. The expression of anger and resentment towards Nakia was very emotional for Sandra. She began the process alone and in writing. This is especially true for survivors of suicide. It took much courage! She felt prodded by both God and me to take these initial steps. The assurance that she received from God and me created a safe haven for her difficult expression. Having a non-judgmental, safe channel (place, outlet, person) that encourages the expression of such pain is very important for the grieving person!

Survivors of suicide experience a complex array of feelings from several contributing factors. Survivors may feel rage toward the deceased for what they feel is a public rejection of them. And this perceived desertion feels like exposing the family's "dirty laundry" in front of the entire world. The survivor may feel that others are judging them as a failure. Anger is often a normal response to enduring, what seems as, public scrutiny and judgment. The survivor often feels the unfairness of their predicament and, as a result, frustration, resentment and anger surface. Feelings of being "victimized" by the deceased is sometimes expressed in survivor statements such as, "Why did she do this to me?", "I'll relive this over and over again and be in pain forever!", and "If she really loved me, she would have thought about how much pain this would cause me!"

A great source of confusion and disillusionment is the anger directed at God. Survivors need to be encouraged to express this anger without feelings of guilt. They need to be reassured that God is quite capable of "handling" our strong emotions and is understanding and loving. Supporting the survivor in clearing this spiritual pathway is important because, very often, it is the path which ultimately leads to peace.

Other sources for anger are blaming others and blaming self. The survivor sometimes feels that if they can find the person who is at fault, it will ease some of the pain and misery. Relationships may become strained, and even fail, at a time when these connections are most important. Blaming is normal in the quest for answering the nagging question of "Why did this happen?" Further, survivors may direct anger at themselves for what they believe that they did or neglected to do to prevent the suicide. This anger is really a form of guilt. Thoughts may proceed as follows: "Maybe I was too hard on her." "Maybe I spoiled her too much." "I should have noticed that something was seriously wrong." "Only if I hadn't left him alone." "I'm not a good mother, father, sister, brother, wife, husband, friend, and person." "I should have listened more." "I didn't love enough." "I loved too much," and on and on and on. These thoughts haunt the survivor because there is no answer or certainty to any of them. This is extremely important - survivors need immediate access to someone they trust and they must have professional help if they begin to repeatedly think negatively about themselves. Hurting oneself won't solve anything and will only further devastate a family already in crisis.

All of this acute hostility needs to come out. If this anger isn't expressed fully and openly, it can add to the length and intensity of pain. There are healthy and productive ways for this to happen. Talking openly to a trusted person who is comfortable with anger and other highly intense emotions is most healing. This person must not try to "downplay" the intensity of what the survivor is feeling, but encourage and accept the survivor's expression of feelings. More importantly, because most adults have been socialized to repress or hide their feelings, and taught that expressing emotions is somehow "bad" or "showing weakness," most of us avoid highly emotional people. If the survivor cannot find an acquaintance or clergy to serve in this role, then seeking professional counseling is an absolute must. Another important connection and resource is the grieving person's medical practitioners. We heal in the context of relationships – with others, the world, and ourselves. God makes these healing relationships available to us. He calls us to love and support each other in this way.

Another primary way of expressing strong emotions is to shed tears. This is a highly effective, yet under utilized venue. We are erroneously told all too often that "big girls and boys don't cry." Well, yes they do! And those who are most mature know how to use their tears effectively to find relief, to heal and to grow. What is the most effective way to use your tears? It is to let them flow freely and in the moment. Stuffing tears means you're stuffing emotions and stuffing emotions leads to further pain. Yes, many people will be uncomfortable with your tears, because they remain unhealed in this area. However, tears are a natural response to hurt and can act as a release and soothing salve to the wounded heart and spirit. Notice how young children move through their tears very quickly and easily and are ready to resume living life. We are all created this way, with a full range of emotions and the natural avenues for expressing them. So, go ahead, cry and sob, with confidence that it is a natural healing process and quite "OK." If you are finding, however, that your tears are not cleansing, that is, you are not feeling relieved or that you are not moving forward in your grief, talk to someone, especially a professional such as a physician or a counselor.

Spiritual practices work miracles in lifting heavy emotions like anger and resentment. This avenue of expression was Sandra's mainstay. Sandra's spiritual practices included morning and evening routines and various outlets during the day when she felt emotionally burdened. Her practices included prayer, reading biblical and other inspirational literature, singing, praise, worship, and various expressions of gratitude, meditations, and conversations with God and herself. Sandra constantly reported the miracles God worked during these times; she received wisdom and guidance, release and relief from pain, and healing for a particular issue, situation and emotion. We were often in awe of the goodness and timeliness of God.

Other ways to ventilate strong emotions are physical exercise, singing, playing a musical instrument, observing and walking in nature, humor and laughing, writing or drawing in a journal, taking a warm bath, and visiting with friends. Even punching pillows and yelling and screaming are appropriate ways to release tension and anger. The point is that all-strong emotions must be acknowledged, expressed and released to regain a sense of balance and wholeness and to move forward along the journey of healing.

My Reflections

"I'm Mad!"

_____

_____

_____

_____

_____

_____

_____

_____

_____

_____

_____

_____

_____

_____

_____

_____

_____

I Have Rest,

Because In Him I'm Blessed

Sometimes I get stressed
And even a little bit depressed
I ask the Lord, "Why is the grass green, and mine is brown?"
I get so mad that sometimes I feel like beating the ground
I cry out to the Lord and scream
Wake me up from this horrible dream
But still I have rest, because in him I'm blessed.
I thought that I had this, but it slipped through my hand
I don't know Lord how much more of this I can stand
My heart is in so much pain
Everything I have is going down the drain
Satan has pushed me to no limit
Why won't you just tell him to shove it
I'm tired, I'm worn, I'm weak
So much so that some things I can't even speak
But I have rest, because in him I'm blessed.
No one understands, they want to, but they're not me
So they just can't see
My thoughts and feelings are still lingering
But people are real encouraging
And because of them I've grown
But I'm still all-alone
Still I have rest, because in him I'm blessed.

I try and I try
My hardest not to cry
But the more I try, I think
Deeper into my heartache and pain I sink
You said you would provide my every need
That if I would follow, you would lead
I've been through the valley of the shadow of death
And every now and then I take a minute to reflect, and then I take
one deep breath
And realize that still I have rest, because in you I'm blessed

Written by Madelyn McCargo
August 1998

Chapter Four

"I'm Lonely!"
Does Anyone Care?

I will never leave thee; Nor forsake thee
Hebrews 13:5

Greater New Mt. Moriah Missionary Baptist Church has to be the greatest Church in the whole world! At least that's the way I felt during the days preceding Nakia's funeral. The outpouring of love that was shown to my family and me was absolutely awesome. I've been at Greater New Mt. Moriah all my life, so with a membership of approximately 1,500 people, quite a few people know my family and me. My Dad, Arthur Murphy Jr., serves as Chairman of the Deacon's Ministry and my husband was also a Deacon at the time of Nakia's death.

News spread quickly that day on **July 15**[th]. A crowd of relatives and friends began to gather outside the house with us, before they took Nakia's body away. Once we were allowed to enter the house, the phones rang constantly; people calling me to ask was it true that Nakia was dead. Within a matter of hours, my house was full of people, mostly my relatives and members of my Church. I remember so well when Nakia's administrator from her job, Pastor Alice Pittman (who also happened to be a friend of mine and a minister), came to the house. There were so many people in the house that she had to take me into the bathroom to talk to me.

My Department of Missions sisters, particularly Circle #14, and several other close friends, devised a plan that I was not to be alone. Nakia's godmother, Linda Bassett, supervised this plan, insisting that someone would be with me at all times. I would awaken each morning to find someone on the couch in the living room, someone in one of the bedrooms and someone curled up in a blanket on the floor. Even when my husband's sisters came in from out of town, my church sisters refused to leave. Every morning breakfast was cooked and all of our needs were met by this wonderful group of women. Linda would leave for a few days to go out of town, but she left explicit instructions that were to be followed to the tee. They were even given instructions that I was to be taken out that Saturday, for a brief walk, shopping, etc., anything that would get me out of the house for a while. I tried to refuse the trip, but was quickly told that the only choice I had in the matter was to decide where I was going, but I was going somewhere. I chose to go to the mall for a little while and I must admit it did help me to get out of the house. My dear friend, Naomi Ruff, took me on this shopping trip, being very attentive to me, and brought me back home when I became tired.

Despite all the attention we received before the funeral, July 22nd came, which was the day after the funeral. I awoke to just a few family members in the house, but the massive influx of traffic to and from the house had ceased. The phone calls slowed down and, in a few days, stopped. I knew life would go back to normal for all of my family and friends, yet, it was a very difficult time for me. I became very depressed and lonely. I didn't seem to know what to do. I prayed and cried a lot. Some of my closest friends would call, usually at the right time, to find me in despair and possibly crying, and they would minister to me. I continue to thank God for loving me so much that it seemed that He would always send someone or have someone to call me at the right time.

The months after the funeral were difficult for me. I knew that I would have some things to go through alone – just God and me. I felt on so many occasions that no one understood my pain. There was no one I could talk to. I missed my talks with Nakia. C. J. and Lynette are quite different from Nakia. Lynette has always been a very private person and C. J. is a young man on the go. My husband was busy with work and school, so I found myself spending most of my time at home alone. Lynette's way of dealing with Nakia's death, was to keep herself busy. She was hardly ever home and when she did come home she usually went straight to bed.

I kept myself quite busy during these days, probably to keep from being alone. My ministry kept me rather busy and, for the most part, I think that was good because it gave me something to do to occupy my time.

It seemed like there were far too many nights that I was alone at home. On these nights, I would just sit and read, or watch television. I found myself longing to see Nakia. I knew this wouldn't happen on this side of eternity, yet, I guess part of me anticipated seeing her.

At this time, Lynette had recently moved out of the house and that was probably a good thing for her. I had mixed feelings about her moving. Although my mind was telling me this was good for Lynette, my emotions were telling me differently. I began to feel all alone, as if I didn't have any daughters left. I started to feel sorry for myself. I began to long for a bond between a mother and daughter that I felt was missing between Lynette and me. I felt cheated out of what I thought I needed as fulfillment as a mother. I knew that this would be an area that I would need God 's help. I started praying, asking God to help me with this. God has been faithful; Lynette and I seem to have grown closer since she moved out. I am trusting God to allow our relationship to blossom into a beautiful relationship between mother and daughter.

When it becomes very hard for me, I try to meditate on the good times that Nakia and I had together. I know I can't have her back and I realize that there are some things I will have to go through alone, but with the help of God I can make it! There are times when I allow God to minister to me through his word and prayer. I try to focus on the fact that the truth of the matter is, I am never really alone. God is always with me, always providing, always meeting my needs, always sending the right people at the right time. I take advantage of my "alone" times by spending time with the Lord in prayer and meditation.

God seems to always provide for me. God has done some awesome things in my life to make sure that I am comforted. He is sealing the bond between Lynette and me. He also has formed a special bond between my stepdaughter Carmen and me. Carmen is the oldest of the girls and she and Nakia had a striking resemblance to each other. They had become very close shortly before Nakia's death. Carmen is working through her grief and is very special to me and God always sends her at the right time.

One of my daughter's best friends just happens to have the same first name as Nakia. She is very much in my life. When Nakia was alive, people always mistook them as "sisters" because of their resemblance to each other. She calls me "mom" and calls my husband "dad." On many occasions, when she is having a hard time or I am having a "moment", she'll come by and we are a help to each other. I don't fully understand it all, but I believe God is covering me with his love and providing the comfort I need.

Monique (my former co-worker) always calls or comes by at the right time. She seems to feel me when I am lonely and God sometimes gives her a word or a vision to share with me. I believe that God has somehow divinely ordained that these three young ladies are a part of my life now. God is covering me with not only the love of my daughter Lynette, but also provides comfort for me through divine providence by allowing these ladies to remind me of Nakia's presence. They are not Nakia, yet, knowing them and their love for Nakia and their resemblance reminds and reinforces for me the truth that Nakia's spirit is very much alive. She is not in them; I sometimes feel her presence around particularly when they are around me.

In my "moments" when I become overwhelmed with the loss of my daughter (I still have my moments and probably always will), I've learned to lean on God for consolation. Psalms 61:1-2 has become a favorite scripture that helps me. I hold to God's promise that I can cast my cares upon him for he cares for me. I try not to dwell on my lonely feelings anymore. Even when the friends and family are not around and I am missing Nakia so... much, I am not alone. How do I know this? God has promised me: *"I will never leave thee, nor forsake thee."* Hebrews 13:5b KJV

Reflections from Carolyn

"I'm Lonely"

Loneliness looms deep and wide in our souls when tragedies strike; our hearts ache with emptiness. Where to go? What to do? Who to call? What meaning does today hold anyway? This feeling of deep despair and loneliness is typical for those who are grieving. It is a tangible deep dark feeling like being in a cave with nothing and no one to console you. You believe that no one could possibly understand the depth of your despair, the intricacies of your grief situation, and the looming fear of going on without the loved one. Life appears too big, to have much too much space, and too void without the physical presence of the loved one. Though there are people, nice people, well-intentioned kind people sent by God's grace, the loneliness of being within one's own skin without the loved one is unbearable!

This description only seems to hint at the overwhelming loneliness experienced by Sandra. She acknowledged and expressed gratitude to God for always sending what seemed to her as people with just the right message, words of kindness or loving act. In spite of these timely visitations, she sensed a deep and very painful loneliness. What Sandra discovered is that in the healing process, which occurs inwardly, you really, are alone. It's God, your grief and you.

Grief is a very personal process. Some general stages have been identified by various "experts" which include shock, denial, relief, catharsis, depression, guilt, preoccupation with the loss, anger, fear, forgiveness, coping, acceptance, and the peace of

95

resolution. However, everyone moves through grief in their own way and in their own timing. There is no clear road map. It is often confusing and the way is complex. Just when you think you've mastered something, settled something, it reappears with a new slant or deeper emotion. The very personal nature of this process can contribute greatly to the loneliness. No one can do the grieving for you and in just the way you need to have it unfold for your healing. However, healing occurs through making rich connections with God, others and you.

Sandra used her resources freely and wisely to help her with her loneliness. What were those resources? We all have them but we may not realize it. They are honesty, spirituality, humility, emotionality, "connect ability" and adaptability. First, she was always honest with herself and others. She openly admitted what she was thinking, feeling and doing, productive and unproductive. Such honesty clears the way for healing. She was able to draw to her just whom or what she needed for the way she was thinking, feeling and acting in each moment. Such admissions allow you to connect with the internal and external resources at the right times. It also allows the spirit to work in and through you in the specific places which need healing. In addition, honesty helps to prevent repression – a denial of or stuffing of our feelings. Sandra's honesty helped her to live into the following scripture: "Ask and you shall receive, seek and ye shall find, knock and the door shall be opened unto you." (Matthew 7:7).

Sandra's spirituality and humility provided her foundation for healing. She maintained a powerful connection with God through consistent spiritual practice. Sandra often spoke of prayer of petition, intercession, thanksgiving, and plain old moans for mercy! Her morning and evening routines consisted of devotions, prayers, meditations, and conversations with God (sometimes she even fussed at Him). She openly shared her most intimate and painful thoughts, feelings and longings. The manner in which Sandra approached her spiritual practice was important. She approached God with humility, yet, with confidence, with faithful expectancy, with trust and with an openness to receive. Sometimes she heard what she wanted, exactly when she wanted it, and other times she didn't. However, she proceeded, trusting what she heard as a real word from God. This brought her much peace, time and time again. Each time she trusted and accepted the comfort and guidance in whatever form it appeared, her relationship with God was strengthened. This

...healing occurs through making rich connections with God, others and you.

strong and ever-renewing relationship with God formed the healing context to her grief. Consequently, through inviting and allowing a free flow between God and her spirit, Sandra's healing was unusually speedy in many areas. As her counselor, I supported her spiritual practice through encouragement and passing on visions and words of wisdom given to me by God. This combination of her practices and my support often worked wonders!

Isolation breeds loneliness, despair and depression. Intuitively Sandra seemed to know this. She possesses what I call a great capacity for "connectivity" and adaptability. What does this mean? Sandra knew when to reach out for help, to whom to reach out, where to reach out, how to reach out, and for what to reach! It's not that she was a genius in this area, but that she allowed her adaptability to flow. She was flexible, open, friendly, expected good, looked for good, and was open to change: her mind, her mood, her surroundings, her company, and so on. This adaptability was a lifesaver for her. Given her ability to change and grasp the goodness from diverse situations and people meant that Sandra was always in a potential healing spot - mentally, spiritually and in the physical world. She never closed down to where healing could come from...she just expected it to come.

My Reflections

"I'm Lonely!

Chapter Five

"I'm Afraid!"
Struggling With Fear

"God has not given us the spirit of fear but of power, love and of a sound mind."　　　**II Timothy 1:7**

The day Nakia died, I experienced fear in a way I had never experienced.. I could not fully verbalize what I feared. My entire being felt afraid, but on that day I didn't have time to dwell on it at all. I had too much to do. I knew I felt different. I felt panicky, sick to the stomach, and unable to sleep, yet, I couldn't stop to assess what was happening. Even after the funeral, I was experiencing moments of fear that I could not explain.

When I began to open up to Carolyn about my fears, many things began to surface. I realized that I was dealing with more than one aspect of fear. I was afraid for my entire family and myself. I struggled with thoughts about myself. For example, "Was I okay?" "Would I lose control emotionally?" "Would I become suicidal?" I had heard of others "losing it" after the death of a loved one – would my family or I be a victim to this "losing it"? "Would my husband be alright?" Charles seemed to internalize his feelings. He is not a very expressive person; therefore, I had no way of measuring if he was coping with Nakia's death. He would not talk about it at all unless I brought it up. I didn't know what he was thinking.

Probably my greatest fears were for Lynette, C. J., Carmen and Tony. These were Nakia's siblings and they were hurting so badly. Tony had even expressed to me that he didn't know how he was going to make it. Carmen felt she had failed Nakia as a big sister. C. J. found Nakia's body - I felt so badly for him. "What could he possibly be thinking and how would he cope?" "Would C. J. be alright or would he one day decide this was all too much for him to handle and end his own life?"

Then, there was Lynette. I was very afraid for her. She and Nakia had a close relationship as sisters. She was hurting so badly. During the family counseling she would barely talk. She wasn't saying much to anyone these days, not even her friends. "Would she become suicidal herself and decide that she didn't want to live without her sister?" She refused to go into counseling, insisting that she was alright. I really battled with my fear for Lynette. I wanted so desperately to help her, yet, she was rejecting any help that came her way. "What could I do?" "How could I help?" "I didn't want to lose another daughter – would she be okay?"

I found myself struggling with such thoughts as: "Is there some hereditary mental illness that runs in my family, causing them to kill themselves?" After all, I had an uncle on my mother's side and an aunt on my husband's side of the family who had completed suicide. "Was there a generational curse on my family?" I had heard people talk about this – I had never thought that I would ever entertain this thought for my own family – yet here I was wondering and afraid.

Some nights it was hard for me to sleep. All these thoughts would run through my mind. There is something eerie about the darkness that multiplies any fears that you already have. The only resource I knew that could help me through this was God. On nights when I couldn't sleep well, I would either lay in the bed praying or get up and get my bible and spend some time in prayer and reading. This seemed to help, particularly as I allowed God to reveal to me others who needed prayer. I learned that when I took the focus off of myself, my own fears, and focused on praying for others, it helped me to make it through "my stuff."

I recognized that this fear was another stage of the grieving process that I would need Carolyn to help me get through. Fear, someone said, is: False Evidence Appearing Real. Carolyn helped me to look at each one of my fears. We tackled each fear,

> *We tackled each fear, taking our time to look at each one, realistically and rationally.*

taking our time to look at each one, realistically and rationally. Carolyn reassured me that I was ok and that just because Nakia took her life, this did not mean that I or the rest of the family were destined to the same fate. My family did not have to be under a generational curse nor did a demon of suicide have control over my family. Carolyn encouraged me to use the tool I use best – prayer! Carolyn did not believe in generational curses and demonic attacks, as this was something she did not conceptualize, but she encouraged me to reach out to my faith in God, believing that God is more powerful than any force in the world and because of His love for me, He would help me.

I realized that prayer was the only answer for me; I had to get through these days, as I prayed for God to remove the fear and to give me peace. I wanted, and asked for, the peace that passeth all understanding. I wanted to trust and believe God for the well-being of my entire family. I knew I had to turn my fears completely over to God. Psalms 55:22 – "Cast your cares on the Lord and he will sustain you, He will never let the righteous fall" - became encouragement to me. I also drew on II Timothy 1:7 for my strength – "God has not given us the Spirit of fear, but of power and of love and of a sound mind." Some days, I would have to quote these scriptures again and again, yet, I was trusting God to get me through this.

I began to relinquish these fears one by one. I was learning more and more about the power of prayer. I thought I knew it, but I soon realized God was taking me to another level in prayer. In December of 1998, while in my bedroom in prayer, God gave me the gift of tongues; I had not asked for it, it just came. As I was praying, a strong sense of urgency came over me, and I began to speak in an unknown language. I now use my "prayer language" often when praying. God uses my languages as a form of intercession for my concerns and for others. I've surrendered my fears to the Lord – trusting Him to take care of my family and me!

Reflections from Carolyn

"I'm Afraid!"
"Struggling with the Fear"

Billy Graham, the well-known evangelist, once said, "As human beings the fear of death appears to be a normal, human response to the unknown. And death, the experience of death, is an unknown." Even as spiritual or religious beings, we have an aversion and fear of death. Gary Kinnaman in his book, *My Companion through Grief*, states that most of us feel that it is not natural to die and that death is the climax of something very wrong in human lives. The fear of death is present in everyone, granted in differing degrees, but nonetheless, a core issue that silently nags and gnaws at each of us, wandering between our conscious and subconscious minds. So when a loved one dies, this event goes straight to our core, bringing up this central fear which impacts us deeply. Death of a loved one by suicide intensifies the depth and complexity of fears.

When a loved one dies, survivors lives are drastically altered and seemingly shattered. Normal routines are no longer normal, and new routines must be developed. Relationships and roles among family members may have to be redefined. Survivors may feel that they are on shaky ground, feeling bizarre and unsure of themselves, and unsure of what the next step should be. They are fearful of what the immediate and distant future holds. At times they are fearful of what the next minute holds for them. They may become fearful of things with which they used to be comfortable. For example, loud noises may cause them to startle, they may experience fear of being alone, fear of new situations, fear that someone else may die, fear of what someone might ask or might say, or perhaps, afraid of the particular room in their home in which the loved one died.

As Sandra stated, she experienced a variety of fears with great intensity. Her greatest fears were of losing control emotionally, i.e. "going crazy", and fear for the safety and mental health of her family members. In light of Nakia's completion of suicide, Sandra's worries were understandable. The magnitude and permanency of the deceased loved one's decision is hard to wrap the mind around and too much for the emotions to contain. This may cause survivors to feel totally out of control, or as if they can't hold onto reality, and that they are experiencing a nightmare. Sandra initially felt terrified, helpless, and like something else "bad" and uncontrollable might happen.

It is very important for the survivor to understand their fear, to know that what they are experiencing is normal and they are not losing their minds. This was crucial for Sandra. She was comforted in knowing that her mind was intact and functioning and that expressing her emotions contributed to her sanity. We have learned incorrectly that if we don't talk about our fears or pretend that our fears don't exist, they will just go away and we will be completely healed. It is just the opposite; healthy healing requires that we understand and conquer fears. Sandra employed major healing strategies for gradually transforming fear into peace. She talked about her anxieties and fears honestly, specifically and consistently. She expressed being afraid for her children because they refused personal counseling and their lack of expressing feelings, and being afraid for her husband's lack of outward expression of emotion. Her fear was that they may become so despondent that they would take their lives as Nakia had. Their silence was very frightening. She also allowed herself to fully feel. She often cried when she ran out of words. She sought consolation and allowed others to minister to her. She never gave up in offering or providing opportunities to her family for counseling, professionally or from other relatives, church members, spiritual colleagues and friends. Sometime she would try a "backdoor" strategy having certain people to interact with her children to find out how they were doing mentally and emotionally! She hasn't given up to this day - not on herself or her family. She remains watchful, hopeful and resourceful.

Most important in Sandra's life is the strength of her connection to God. Her faith in the goodness and power of God sustains her. Fear and faith just don't mix. Fear cannot operate fully in the same space. Sandra activated her faith through an active and intense prayer life. She relied heavily on the promise that "God has not given us the spirit of fear, but of power, and of love, and of a sound mind (II Timothy 1:7). She truly believes this. What is phenomenal about Sandra is her ability to find congruency (a tying together) between her mental health practices and her religion. For example, while Sandra believes in this scripture with all her heart, she also believes that God ordains people to help us to regain and live into our power, to discover that we are love and loved, and to grab a hold of and use our sound minds! While Sandra would be the first to admit that she is not totally without fear, she has come a long way in her journey for peace.

Kinnaman, Gary. *My Companion Through Grief, Comfort For Your Darkest Hour.* Vine Books, Servant Publications: Ann Arbor, MI. 2004

My Reflections

"I'm Afraid!"

_____

_____

_____

_____

_____

_____

_____

_____

_____

_____

_____

_____

_____

_____

Oh Bliss,
It's Wonderful to be in Your Midst

Happy am I to be one of yours
The one whom everyone adores
I love you Lord, more and more
Some people say, "Oh you're a Christian, your life must be a bore"
I say, "No you've got it all wrong, I'm happy, I'm glad,
And thank the Lord, I'm not even sad."
And oh listen to this
Oh bliss, it' wonderful to be in your midst.
Oh rejoice, rejoice
Can't you hear his voice?
You see Jesus speaks to me Even on my stormy sea
He hears my faintest cry
And yes, he'll answer by and by
Heartache and pain, they only last for a time
But rejoice, rejoice, for you are one of mine
Oh bliss, it's wonderful to be in your midst.
You are so wonderful and so kind
My shattered broken heart you will bind
Your love forever will abound.
And your blessed presence is all around
"And when ever Gabriel trumpet may sound
Come unto me and receive your crown,
Look up to me
And see don't you see
My glory shine
For here with me is one of mine
Oh bliss, It's wonderful to have you here in my midst.

Madelyn McCargo

Chapter Six

"Peace in the Midst Of!"

"And the peace of God, which passeth all understanding, shall keep your heart and mind through Christ Jesus"   *Philippians 4:7*

It has been nearly eight years, now, since Nakia took her life. My counseling sessions with Carolyn have long ago ended. We only see each other now on special occasions and to work on this book. I will always be grateful to God and Carolyn. I know that I am where I am today because of her obedience and love for God, and her willingness to counsel me. We both have gone on with our lives: me with my preaching/teaching ministry and Carolyn with her counseling. We try and connect with each other at least once a month, just to see what's happening because God is doing such an awesome thing in both of our lives. Carolyn will always be a part of my life – I will never, ever forget her and somehow, I know God will continue to use the both of us – sometimes together, to assist in the healing of so many hurting people.

I still have my "moments" when I miss my Nakia so much, but they are not as often, now. Yes, there are still some "moments that I feel the pain so intensely," yet, I am able to work it through. I made the decision (with the help of God and

Carolyn), to go on with my life. I am trying to allow God to use me in whatever way He wants me for His Glory. I know that I have a tremendous peace about Nakia's death now. I find my peace in knowing that I will one day see Nakia again – "absent from the body present with the Lord." I hold on to this, but until my journey here on this side of eternity ends – I have work to do, I have a journey to complete so I must complete the tasks that God has given me.

I am fully aware that God is doing a "quick" thing in my life. Since Nakia's death, the following has occurred in my life – all to the glory of God: On December 30, 1998, I preached my first sermon and was licensed to preach the Gospel by my Pastor, the Reverend Kenneth James Flowers and my church, Greater New Mt. Moriah Missionary Baptist Church. In April of 1999, the Yellow Ribbon Suicide Prevention Detroit Chapter was founded by Brenda Walker, Chairperson and myself as Co-Chairperson. On May 7, 2000, I was ordained into the Gospel Ministry by Pastor, and probably the most awesome thing in my life right now, is that on August 1, 2001, I left my job of 15 ½ years to minister on a full-time basis at Greater New Mt. Moriah as the Assistant to Pastor Flowers – I truly serve an AWESOME GOD!

My days are quite busy. I enjoy my ministry and I am in awe of God and all he is doing in my life. Greater New Mt. Moriah has a membership of approximately 1200 people so there is always something to do: teaching, preaching, funerals, weddings, meetings, etc. Pastor Flowers has truly been a blessing to my ministry. He keeps me quite busy – he is a very busy Pastor and I praise God daily for him and for God allowing me to be his Assistant! I have an incredible need to preach, with which God helps me. God has given me a "prophetic ministry" and on many occasions God has "sent" me to other churches to "proclaim the word of God."

Brenda and I, and the committee, have done several suicide prevention workshops. We have even had a couple of television and newspaper interviews. I also did a taping with a group of survivors of suicide that has been shown to high schools across America. I consider suicide prevention to be a major part of my ministry. My ministry is not just to preach, but also to minister to others, the best I can; and part of that is done by getting the message out to others, young and old, that there is help instead of despair in times of trouble. Every chance I get, I tell others of the love of God and that God desires to help us: "Cast your burdens upon the Lord, and he shall sustain thee; he shall never suffer the righteous to be moved." Psalms 55:22. I also encourage those who need professional help to go and get the help they need. God ordains and anoints counselors. God wants us to be healed so that we can do the work he has purposed for us. I am very open about how God used Carolyn to counsel me and I am a great proponent of professional counseling.

I pray that someone has been helped by me sharing my story of how God walked me through a very difficult time in my life. I especially desire those who read this book to know that God is more than able to provide the help that we need. If we need professional help – we should get it and not be ashamed! Most of all, if I could pass on one thing to someone else, it would be this encouragement:

Allow God to move you from pain to comfort; trust God to turn your sorrow and pain into peace and joy – a peace that passeth all *understanding and a joy in knowing that you will see <u>your loved one again</u>.*

May God's grace, love and peace forever shine upon you!!

My Final Reflections

"Peace in the Midst of

_____

_____

_____

_____

_____

_____

_____

_____

_____

_____

_____

_____

_____

_____

Afterword

by
Matthew Parker
President, Institute for Black Family Development

The love between a parent and child is a precious experience. This book captures the joy of motherhood, the pride of a child's accomplishments, the grief and inner pain of life lost, and the healing, restoration and forgiveness that comes with time.

This book is the journey of two African American women who have shared their lives with each other. The quality and character that they demonstrate will be an encouragement to all readers. As you read this book, it is my desire that you would begin to share these experiences with others.

The Bible says, *"In this you greatly rejoice, though now for a little while you may have had to suffer grief in all kinds of trials. These have come so that your faith of greater worth than gold, which perishes even though refined by fire may be proved genuine and may result in praise, glory and honor when Jesus Christ is revealed."*

I Peter 1: 6-7

APPENDIX
Suggested Scripture Readings

Old Testament
Deuteronomy 31: 6
Psalm 23
Psalm 50: 15
Psalm 61: 1-2
Psalms 91
Psalm 116: 1-2
Psalm 119
Psalm 121
Proverbs 3: 5-6
Isaiah 26: 3-4
Isaiah 41: 10
Jeremiah 33: 3
Lamentations 3: 22-24

New Testament
Matthew 6: 25-34
Matthew 11: 28
II Corinthians 1: 3-4
Philippians 4: 6-7
I Thessalonians 4: 13-18
II Timothy 1: 7
Hebrews 4: 14-16
I Peter 5: 8-10

**Resources

National Suicide Prevention Lifeline
1-800-799-4889 | www.suicidepreventionlifeline.org/

Suicide Prevention Response Center
1-800-273-TALK | www.sprc.org/

National Crisis Hotlines and Helplines
Consult directory assistance

Numbers subject to change

Biography

Rev. Sandra Kay Gordon, BRE

Rev. Sandra K. Gordon is a product of the Detroit Public School System, graduating from Cass Technical High School. She attended Ferris State College where she became a charter member of Alpha Kappa Alpha Sorority, Zeta Epsilon Chapter. Rev. Gordon graduated Cum Laude from William Tyndale College in 1988 where she received a Bachelors of Religious Education Degree with a major in Urban Studies. She is currently pursuing a Master of Divinity degree from Ecumenical Theological Seminary.

Rev. Gordon has attended Greater New Mt. Moriah Missionary Baptist Church all of her life. It is there where she received Christ and has been a member since the age of 8. She attributes much of who she is today to the teaching and guidance she received from those who have mentored her throughout the years. Rev. Gordon has always felt a tremendous need to serve and minister to others. She has served for over 20 years in the Teaching Ministry and Youth Ministry of the Church. She has served at Greater New Mt. Moriah as Superintendent for the Youth Division of Sunday School, Chairperson for Circle 14 Department of Missions, and Interpreter for the Hearing Impaired.

Rev. Gordon received her call into the Preaching Ministry on January 26, 1997. She announced her call to the Church on April 12, 1998. She preached her first sermon and was licensed to preach on December 30, 1998 by the church and her Pastor and Father in the ministry, the Reverend Kenneth James Flowers. She was ordained on May 7, 2000.

In June of 2000, at the Annual Benjamin L. Hooks Image Awards Banquet, Rev. Gordon received the Humanitarian Award from her Church. In March of 2001 Rev. Gordon received recognition from the Cit`e D'etroit Top Ladies of Distinction at their African American Women in Ministry Luncheon.

Rev. Gordon is also active in the Michigan Progressive Baptist Convention (MPBC), formerly having served as Youth Director and Divisional Vice President of the Division of Christian Education. She currently serves as 2nd Vice President of the Ministers Council.

Rev. Gordon ministers to many women who struggle with their call. She is considered by many to be a mid-wife; one who helps birth ministries in women. Feeling a strong need to help women identify their calls and to fellowship with other women ministers, Rev. Gordon organized and founded the Daughters of Deborah - Women in Ministry Fellowship in August of 1999. This is an ecumenical women's fellowship group that meets monthly to encourage women in ministry.

After the suicide of her own daughter, Nakia, in July of 1998, God began to use Rev. Gordon to minister to hurting people. The Yellow Ribbon Suicide Prevention Program - Detroit Chapter, was formed in March of 2000 by Chairperson Brenda Walker, where Rev. Gordon served for six years as Co-

Chairperson. Rev. Gordon has spoken and taught workshops on suicide prevention in the Detroit area, at Churches, Health-O'Ramas and many other organizations. Rev. Gordon feels compelled to reach others with a message of hope instead of despair. Rev. Gordon and counselor Carolyn McKanders have recently released their book together to minister to hurting people.

On August 1, 2001 Rev. Gordon left her job of 15 ½ years to go into full time ministry at Greater New Mt. Moriah working as Assistant to the Pastor – To God be the Glory!. She also leads the Intercessory Prayer Team at Greater New Mt. Moriah and teaches in the Church School Adult division.

In January 2008, Rev. Gordon was selected along with other clergy, business and social activists to be a part of an African American Leaders Mission to Israel. This was an Educational Tour of Israel sponsored by the American Israel Public Affairs Committee, (AIPAC).

Rev. Gordon is married to Rev. Charles E. Gordon. They have two children, Sandra Lynette and Charles Jr. (C.J.) She is the daughter of Deacon Arthur Murphy Jr.-Chairman of the Deacon's Ministry at Greater New Mt. Moriah.

Rev. Gordon desires to be used of the Lord to minister to the needs of the people, and to proclaim the Gospel of our Lord and Savior Jesus Christ.

To contact Rev. Gordon or for more information:

Rev. Sandra K. Gordon
c/o PriorityONE Publications
P.O. Box 725 ▪ Farmington, MI 48332
skgordon@p1pubs.com
(313) 399-8699

$\mathcal{B}iography$

Carolyn M. McKanders, MSW

A Joyful Servant

Spiritual Teacher and Counselor

Spiritual teaching and counseling are experiences that help us to discover the Truth about ourselves; they enable us to understand and feel our spiritual identity- one of love, beauty and wholeness. These experiences help us to ask and answer some of life's most challenging questions about which we often wonder. They teach us that our resources are God-given and mainly internal and seek to connect us to these resources- returning us to Love. Knowing who we are grounds us and brings peace and balance, enabling us to heal more quickly, forgive more readily, and love ourselves and others more completely. *And the Truth shall make you free* (John 8:32). Carolyn counsels, teaches and facilitates spiritual retreats.

Educational Consultant

Carolyn McKanders is an international educational consultant specializing in individual, group and organizational development. Carolyn's passion is promoting quality human relationships through communication, collaboration, and leadership skills development. Over the past five years she has worked as an independent consultant providing staff development through presentations, group facilitation, and instructional and leadership coaching. Her expertise includes providing polarity management training that helps organizations identify and manage competing tensions inherent in social systems. Carolyn's background includes 28 years of experience in Detroit Public Schools as a teacher, counselor and staff development specialist.

Carolyn earned a Bachelor of Science degree in Child Development and Education from Michigan State University; a Master of Arts in Counseling and Education from the University of Michigan; and a Master of Social Work degree in Family and Child Services from Eastern Michigan University.

She is blessed with a loving, supportive husband, Kenneth McKanders, J.D. and four phenomenal children: Kimberly McKanders, M.D., Karla McKanders, J.D., Kristal McKanders, M.A. and Kenny, a high school senior.

Carolyn expresses gratitude to God, the Source of all and within all. Her wish is to express love, peace and wisdom fully as a joyful servant!

To contact Carolyn McKanders or for more information:

Carolyn McKanders, MSW
c/o PriorityONE Publications
P.O. Box 725 • Farmington, MI 48332
cmckanders@p1pubs.com
(313) 378-5078

BOOK ORDER FORM

Nakia's Gift:

A Mother's Journey from Misery to Ministry
By Rev. Sandra K. Gordon & Carolyn M. McKanders, MSW

Name _____

Address _____

City _____ State _____ Zip _____

Phone _____ Fax _____

Email _____

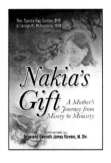

Quantity	
Price *(each)*	$15.99
Subtotal	
S & H *(each)*	$2.99
MI Tax 6%	
TOTAL	

METHOD OF PAYMENT:

❑ Check or Money Order (***Make payable to***: PriorityONE Publications)

❑ Visa ❑ Master Card ❑ American Express

Acct No. _____

Expiration Date *(mmyy)* _____ CVV _____

Signature _____

Mail your payment with this form to:

PriorityONE Publications
P. O. Box 725
Farmington, MI 48332
(800) 596-4490 – Toll Free
URL: http://www.p1pubs.com
Email: info@p1pubs.com